Harvard Documents
in the History of Education

PUBLISHED UNDER THE DIRECTION OF
THE GRADUATE SCHOOL OF EDUCATION

London: Humphrey Milford

OXFORD UNIVERSITY PRESS

The
Public Schools of Colonial Boston
1635-1775

By

ROBERT FRANCIS SEYBOLT

PROFESSOR OF THE HISTORY OF EDUCATION
UNIVERSITY OF ILLINOIS

Cambridge
HARVARD UNIVERSITY PRESS
1935

118645

PRINTED IN THE UNITED STATES OF AMERICA
BY D. B. UPDIKE, THE MERRYMOUNT PRESS
BOSTON, MASSACHUSETTS

TO

JULIUS HERBERT TUTTLE

A SMALL TOKEN OF

MY AFFECTION AND ADMIRATION

FOREWORD

WITH the exception of the first "Free schoole," the public schools of colonial Boston have received but little attention. Here and there in the writings on early Boston the names of the other schools are mentioned, but that is all. The most extensive treatment, which contains but little in addition to its chronological lists of masters and ushers at the various schools, would not fill two octavo pages. Incidentally, the lists are inaccurate with respect to names as well as dates.

In a publication of 1911 it is said that "By 1682 the school established in 1635 had become so crowded that two others were established, 'to teach children to write and cipher.' . . . These, and others established later, became the so-called Grammar Schools of Boston, wherein masters taught reading, spelling, grammar, geography, and the 'higher branches.' " This looks as if it might have been inspired by a statement published eleven years earlier: "In 1682 . . . it was ordered in town meeting: 'That a committee with the selectmen consider and provide for the teaching of children to write and cipher within this town.' Accordingly, grammar schools were soon opened, with one department for teaching 'writing and ciphering,' and another department for teaching 'reading and spelling.' . . . These grammar schools of 1682, however, were open to boys only." I can discover no other source for it.

So far, these two statements have gone unchallenged. As a matter of fact, no public schools of any sort were established in 1682. The second public school, the *writing school* in Prison Lane (later Queen Street) was opened November 1, 1684. Until April 20, 1713, when the North Grammar School was opened, the "Free schoole" of 1635 was the only public "grammar school" in Boston. At no time did the former offer anything but the usual program of instruction in Latin and Greek.

Much has been said about the first Public Latin School, and much of it is not so. Brief samples, from publications of 1929 and 1934, will suffice. "The first successful attempt to establish a Latin grammar school in this country was made in Boston in 1635 from funds subscribed by forty-five contributors." These "funds" were not subscribed until August 12, 1636. Commenting on "The Latin grammar schools . . . in New England," the author states that "They were generally planned, supported, and managed by the classes and not in the interest of the masses. The students paid tuition fees." Both statements are incorrect, as far as the Boston public grammar schools are concerned. Another writer says that Ezekiel Cheever was "a graduate of Cambridge, England." He was not.

The "standard" treatise since 1886, H. F. Jenks's *Catalogue of the Boston Public Latin School. . . . With an historical sketch*, is not wholly reliable. However, impressed by its great mass of detail, in text and citation of sources, many writers have depended on it for their "facts."

This little study is an attempt to present, in compact form, a verifiable account of the public schools of colonial Boston, the beginnings of the school system which celebrates its three hundredth anniversary April 13, 1935. For this purpose, all available manuscript and printed records have been examined. Nothing has been read into them: they tell their story without urging. If the account is not complete, the materials will permit but little more. I have not drawn upon my imagination, nor have I used any of the numerous unsupported legends and anecdotes, to fill the gaps. The book is designed for those who are interested in documentary sources. It may also be useful to one who would essay the more felicitous, definitive history of the Boston public school system.

The sources include manuscript documents in the Massachusetts Archives (at the State House), Boston City Hall, Massachusetts Historical Society, Harvard College Library, New England Historic Genealogical Society, the Public Latin School library, and the Suffolk County Probate Records. Text and notes will reveal, also, the use that has been made of colony enactments, early Boston newspapers, diaries, letter-books, ledgers, maps, family line-books, the vital records of the Massachusetts towns, gravestones in the Copp's Hill, Granary, King's Chapel, and Common burying grounds, and books of epitaphs. The minutes of the town meetings and the selectmen's meetings are the chief sources of information.

It should be noted that the printed town records are not, in every instance, faithful transcriptions of the original. Furthermore, the index-citations are neither complete nor accurate. The town clerks, themselves, were not always reliable. Names and dates were often entered incorrectly.

CONTENTS

CHAPTER   PAGE

   I. THE SCHOOLS   1

  II. MASTERS AND USHERS OF THE GRAMMAR SCHOOLS   12

 III. MASTERS AND USHERS OF THE WRITING SCHOOLS   21

 IV. APPOINTMENTS AND QUALIFICATIONS   28

  V. SUPPORT   33

 VI. SALARIES AND ALLOWANCES   43

VII. SUPERVISION   57

VIII. STUDIES   67

APPENDIX

  A. LIST OF SALARIES   79

  B. EZEKIEL CHEEVER'S DWELLING   89

  C. SCHOOL VISITORS, JULY 1, 1761   91

  D. SOURCES FOR ENROLLMENT STATISTICS   93

  E. ADDENDA   96

INDEX OF NAMES   99

CHAPTER I
THE SCHOOLS

THE earliest reference to a public school in Boston is to be found in the minutes of a town meeting of April 13, 1635, at which it "was then generally agreed upon y^t o^r brother Mr Philemon Pormort shalbe intreated to become scholemaster for the teaching and nourtering of children wth us."[1] Records of later date do not indicate whether the school was opened in 1635. There can be no doubt of its establishment, however, shortly after "a general meeting of the richer inhabitants," August 12, 1636, who pledged a sum of money sufficient to guarantee the first year's salary for "a free school master of the youth."[2]

It is very probable that, during the early years, the school was conducted in the homes of the masters.[3] The first building was erected on the "way from Haugh^s Corner Leading North westerly . . . extending as far as M^rs. Whetcombs Corner."[4] It seems to have met the needs of the town until 1655, when the selectmen were instructed "to lay outt a peece of Ground" for "the building of a house for instruction of the

[1] For this historic record, I have used the manuscript volume, *Records of the Town of Boston*, 1634–1660, preserved at the City Hall. It should be noted that here (B. R., II, 5), and in many other instances, the printed records of the town are not faithful transcriptions of the original. The chirography is not always easy to decipher.

The abbreviation B. R. is employed throughout to indicate Boston Records, i.e. *Reports of the Record Commissioners of the City of Boston*.

Adjourned meeting dates are used when indicated by the records.

[2] B. R., II, 160.

[3] Pormort lived on the west side, near the south corner, of a lane (called Church Square, 1708; Cornhill Square, 1809; Cornhill Court, 1814) which ran from Cornhill (now Washington Street) westerly, then northerly, then easterly, returning to Cornhill opposite King (now State) Street. This lane ran around the second building (erected 1640) of the First Church, which stood on the site now occupied by the building at 209 Washington Street. A location-tablet might be placed on the door of the dining-room entrance to the old Young's Hotel.

Maude lived on the west side of the "Highway leading from Prison lane up to the Common" (now Tremont Street), somewhat south of the site marked by the tablet on Pemberton Square.

Woodbridge's home cannot be located in the town deeds. See p. 96, *infra*.

[4] Contemporary records do not supply the date of construction. A schoolhouse, separate from the master's dwelling, is mentioned for the first time in a record of Mar. 29, 1652 (B. R., II, 109; X, 84). It stood at the rear of the site now occupied by King's Chapel (original building, 1688). Woodmansey's dwelling, owned by the town, was east of the schoolhouse, separated from it by a small plot.

In the early days, this "way" was called "School house lane," or "School House Street." It was named "School Street," May 3, 1708 (B. R., VIII, 51).

youth of the town."[5] Within a few years, it was found that the school was too small to accommodate adequately the number of pupils enrolled. On January 30, 1664/65, the selectmen voted the "inlardgment of the Towne schoole-house."[6] Evidently they estimated well, for it was almost forty years before the town voted to build "a New School House . . . in Stead of the Old School House."[7] The selectmen, instructed by the town "to get the Same accomplished," appointed a committee "to advise there about," and to consult with the master and usher concerning certain details of construction.[8] Early in the summer of 1704, the old "School-House was taken down and a more comodious one" was ready for occupancy in October.[9] Samuel Sewall, in a letter to Jeremiah Dummer, October 10, 1704, says: "I did not tell you that last Satterday after noon I went to Mr. Chiever, and having a fair occasion, said to him how well pleased I was with the building of a New School-house, and that it would be very convenient for him to be saluted with a good Latin Oration at his entrance into it. But he seemed to reject it with some Indignation, and spoke of your mentioning of it to Mr. Williams."[10]

In this connection, it may not be inappropriate to reproduce the contract with the builder: "Agreed wth M^r. John Barnerd as followeth, he to build a new School House of forty foot Long, Twenty-five foot wide & Eleven foot Stud, with eight windows below & five in the Roofe with wooden Casements to the eight Windows, to Lay the lower flowr with Sleepers & double boards So far as needfull, & the Chamber flowr with

<hr>

[5] B. R., II, 129 (Mar. 14, 1655/56). See also B. R., II, 132 (Dec. 29, 1656). This building was erected on the old site.

[6] B. R., VII, 24.

[7] B. R., VIII, 31 (Mar. 13, 1703/4).

[8] B. R., XI, 38–39 (June 27, 1704). It is probable that, during the period of construction, the students attended "at the Town house in the Representatives Room." This arrangement was made June 25, 1721, when it was reported to the selectmen that there were "Several Persons in Distinct Houses in School Street near to the Publick Gramer Scholl sick of the Small pox which may Prevent many of the youth attending the School at that Place" (B. R., XIII, 83).

[9] B. R., XI, 42 (Jan. 29, 1704/5): The selectmen voted that "the Congregation of French Protestants," which, since 1687, "had their Publick meetings for the worship of God in the Free School-House," might "have the liberty to meet" in the new building "as formerly they did in the Old."

The congregation of the First Church (destroyed by fire, Oct. 2, 1711) was permitted, Dec. 17, 1711, to use the schoolhouse, after five o'clock, "as they Shall have Ocation during their present want of a Meeting House" (B. R., XI, 152). A new meeting house (the Old Brick) was erected in the following year.

[10] The Letter-Book of Samuel Sewall, in *Coll. Mass. Hist. Soc.*, 6th Series, I, 302. Nathaniel Williams was usher to Ezekiel Cheever.

Single boards, to board below the plate inside & inside and out, to Clapboard the Out side and Shingle the Roof, to make a place to hang the Bell in, to make a paire of Staires up to the Chamber, and from thence a Ladder to the bell, to make one door next the Street, and a partition Cross the house below & to make three rows of benches for the boyes on each Side of the Room, to finde all Timber, boards, Clapboards, Shingles, nayles, hinges. In consideration whereof the S^d. M^r. John Barnerd is to be paid One hundred pounds, and to have the Timber, Boards & Iron worke of the Old School House."[11] This is the only known contemporary description of the new building.

Early in the year 1748, "the Minister Wardens and Vestry" of King's Chapel, planning "to Rebuild said Church and make it some what larger," petitioned the town for a grant of land; "and whereas the Town" had "a School house upon part of the Land," the petitioners offered to "Purchase and make over to the Town a Peice of Ground" for a new building, remarking "that the said Grant will be no detriment to the Town as the present School house is much decayed in many parts defective, and will in a Short Space of time require to be New Built."[12] The land offered to the town was "over against the present Grammer School . . . measuring 34½ feet thereabouts on School Street and running 97 feet back more or less," on which the petitioners agreed "to Erect . . . a New School house of like Dimensions and accomodations with the present and finish the same in like decent manner to the Satisfaction of the Selectmen; unless the Pet^rs. should propose a Sum of Money to the Acceptance of the Town, instead of Erecting the said Building."[13] This offer, embodied in a town committee report, was accepted by the town, April 18, 1748.[14] At a meeting of June 29, 1748, the chairman of the King's Chapel committee "made an offer to the Select men that if they would Build the Grammer School," he would

---

[11] B. R., XI, 39–40 (July 24, 1704), 41–42 (Oct. 30, 1704).

[12] B. R., XIV, 144–45 (Apr. 11, 1748). Earlier, unsatisfactory petitions had been withdrawn: B. R., XIV, 135–36 (Mar. 15, 1747/48), 140 (Mar. 28, 1748), 143 (Apr. 4, 1748).

[13] B. R., XIV, 147 (Apr. 18, 1748).

[14] B. R., XIV, 148 (Apr. 18, 1748). The close vote of 205 to 197 was "brought in" after an unusually stormy meeting, at which one John Pigeon was "observed . . . to put in about a dozen with the word Yea wrote on all of 'em," for which he paid a fine of £5 "for putting in more than one Vote according to Law."

On April 30, 1748 (B. R., XVII, 192), the selectmen accepted, from the King's Chapel committee, the deed to the land for the new school. John Tyng, who voted against accepting it, insisted on having his vote recorded, May 4, 1748 (B. R., XVII, 192–93).

"Pay them or their order" £2400 "old tenor."[15] On this the selectmen voted "in the Negative."[16]

The building on which the selectmen agreed was "A Brick house of the Dimensions following, Vizt. Thirty four feet front towards School street, Thirty six feet deep on the Passage and twelve feet stud."[17] At a meeting of May 3, 1749, a spokesman of the King's Chapel committee "informed the Select men that every thing was Compleated at the new School house by them Built for the use of the Town, and therefore desired that the Scholars may be removed out of the old School-house, into the New, that so the said Committee may go to Work in laying the Foundation of their Church," whereupon it was voted that the "Master of the South Grammer School, be directed to remove his Scholars into the New School house, on Monday morning next being the Eighth of May instant."[18]

Except for the period during which the town was occupied by British soldiers, this building was in continuous use throughout the eighteenth century. Recalling the day on which the school was closed, Harrison Gray Otis said: "On the 19th of April, 1775, I went to school for the last time. In the morning about seven, Percy's brigade was drawn up extending from Scollay's building thro' Tremont Street nearly to the bottom of the Mall, preparing to take up their march for Lexington. A corporal came up to me as I was going to school, and turned me off to pass down Court St. which I did, and came up School St. to the School-house. It may well be imagined that great agitation prevailed, the British line being drawn up a few yards only from the School house door. As I

[15] B. R., XVII, 197. The final cost was £2700 old tenor.

[16] B. R., XVII, 198.

[17] B. R., XVII, 198–99 (July 20, 1748). An interesting supplement to this brief description appears in a petition from John Lovell, the master, May 21, 1772, in which he calls attention to his "interest & care in procuring Subscriptions for further Conveniences & Ornaments to the School House, than the Contractors were obliged to furnish: The Effects of which appear in the hight of the Walls of the Room two feet above what the Masons were to build them by Contract in the Carvings round the top, the Frontispeice of the Doors, the Cornish round the Pediment & Eves; the Cupola for the Bell with the Fane upon the top, & the large & commodious Stone Steps at the Entrance of the School" (B. R., XVIII, 81). See also B. R., XIV, 208 (Mar. 9, 1751/52): "Voted that a Porch be built at the South Entrance of the Grammer School."

[18] B. R., XVII, 218. On Mar. 6, 1748/49, the King's Chapel committee reported to the selectmen that "the School house by them Erected on the South Side of School Street . . . is now finished" (B. R., XVII, 212). It stood at the west corner of Cook's Court (Chapman Place), on the land now occupied by the Parker House.

The French Congregation was again given permission, Mar. 15, 1748/49, "to Meet in the said School house" (B. R., XVII, 213).

entered I heard the announcement of 'deponite libros' and ran home for fear of the regulars."[19] At a meeting of the selectmen, June 5, 1776, it was "Voted, that the Grammar School in School Street be opened."[20]

For almost a half century, from the date of its establishment, this was the only public school in Boston. Town records refer to it as "the Schoole," or "the Free schoole," until November 1, 1684, when the first public writing school was opened.[21] It was then called "the Latine School," or "the Free Grammer School."[22] After the North Grammar School was opened April 20, 1713, the old "Free schoole" was called the "South Grammar School."[23]

At a town meeting, December 18, 1682, the selectmen were instructed "to consider of & pvide one or more Free Schooles for the teachinge of Children to write & Cypher within this towne."[24] The outcome of their deliberation was a vote, April 30, 1683, "that Two schooles shall be pvided."[25] No further reference to these schools appears in the town records until November 24, 1684, when two of the selectmen "made a returne y[t] accordinge to a former ord[r] they had agreed with John Cole to keep a Free schoole to teach y[e] Children of the Towne to read & write for one year from the 1st of this instant Nov[r]."[26] Apparently, only one school was established at this time; and it may have been discontinued for a period after the expiration of John Cole's one year appointment.[27] However, Cole was in charge of the school from March 10, 1689/90 to April 12, 1714.[28]

On March 8, 1696/97, the town "Voted that there be a hous built

[19] Jenks, H. F., *Catalogue of the Boston Public Latin School, established in 1635. With an historical sketch* (Boston, 1886), "Hist. Sketch," 37.

[20] B. R., XXV, 2.

[21] B. R., II, 82, 95, 124, 133, 142; VII, 22, 33, 38, 57, 63, 151. It is called "the grammer schoole" in but one record, Mar. 26, 1666 (B. R., VII, 30).

[22] B. R., VII, 234, 236, 244; VIII, 7, 28, 29, 34, 51, 63, 64, 75, 76, 78, 80, 81, 90. Earlier habit persisting, it was referred to as "the Free schoole" in 1685 and 1709 (B. R., VII, 177; VIII, 63).

[23] Until 1789. Nowhere in the town records of the seventeenth and eighteenth centuries is it called the "Boston Latin School." The present official designation is the "Public Latin School."

[24] B. R., VII, 158.

[25] B. R., VII, 161.

[26] B. R., VII, 171.

[27] It is not mentioned in the records of the next five years.

[28] B. R., VII, 200 (Mar. 10, 1689/90). The phrasing, "Ordered That Mr John Cole be allowed to keep a Free schoole for reading and writing & y[t] y[e] Select men agree with him for his salery," indicates a reappointment. See also B. R., XI, 202 (Apr. 13, 1714).

for the Writing school adjoining to the old school house, it is to be left with the select men."[29] A letter from Sewall to Increase Mather, July 24, 1688, places the old schoolhouse in Prison Lane. Town records of 1698–1699 refer to "the New School house at Cotton Hill," and "the School house Lately Built in the Prison lane on the side of the hill over against the Land of Capt Sam^{ll} Sewall."[30] From 1708 to 1788, this school was known as the "Writing School in Queen Street."

Although the minutes of town and selectmen's meetings contain no record of its existence, there was a "Publick Schoole" at the "North End" of Boston, in 1687. Two interesting documents are our only sources of information concerning this school. One, bearing no date, is "The Humble Petition of Joshua Natstock of Boston," addressed to Governor Andros:

Whereas the Chief Inhabitants of the North end of the Town of Boston have invited yor Petitioner to take upon him the care and Managem^t as mast^r of a free Schoole (it being now Destitute) And have as by their annexed Certificate recommended him to the Aprobation of the Selectmen, But yor Petition^r being unwilling to undertake any place of Publique trust without yor Excell^{cies} Favour and direction first had and known. To wch yor petitioner as in Duty bound doth humble referr himself in this matt^r And most humbly prayes y^t your Excell^{cie} would be pleased to favour him with a Licence to instruct Youth in the School as abovesd, in wch your Petition^r Shall make itt his care and Study to perform w^t to his Duty in Such an undertaking doth belong.[31]

[29] B. R., VII, 226.

[30] B. R., VII, 232 (Dec. 20, 1698), 233 (Jan. 30, 1698/99). See also B. R., XII, 100 (July 11, 1722): "the School house at the uper End of Queen Street."

Prison Lane (Queen Street, 1708; Court Street, 1788) ran from Cornhill (now Washington Street), opposite King (now State) Street, westerly and northerly to the head of Hanover Street. The schoolhouse stood within the lane, on a lot approximately where the present south entrance to the subway at Scollay Square is located. This lot was at the southern end of an elongated, island-like plot. The location is definitely indicated in the report of a survey requested by Samuel Sewall, Dec. 20, 1698 (B. R., VII, 232): "The Distance from the Southerly Corner of the New School house at Cotton Hill to the North^{ly} Corner of Capt Leggs Land is 55 foot, from s^d N^{ly}. corner of s^d school house to the South^{ly} post of Capt Sewells gate, Being the Breadth Cross the high way is 53 foot 4 inches, from s^d gate post to the South Easterly end of the school house fence, neere the dore of s^d Schoolhouse is 41 foot & a halfe. The Breadth of the uper highway between Mr. Coney & Belknap on the one side & Capt Sewells Land on the other side is 17 foot. From the Easterly corner of the School house Cross the high way to the N.W. gate post of the house late of Mr Pirkis is 36 foot. From the E. corner of s^d school house to the N. corner of the Land formerly belonging to Mr John Mears Deceased 11 pole & one foot. From s^d N. corner Cross the high way to Capt Bozoon Allens Land is 25 foote and a halfe."

Enlargements were voted in 1715, 1750, and 1753.

[31] *Massachusetts Archives* (Usurpation Papers), CXXVII, 25.

It may be inferred, from the omission of his name from the minutes of town and selectmen's meetings, that he was unable to secure the appointment from either body. He turned, therefore, to Governor Andros who was well known for actions contrary to the "custom" of the town. The reply follows:

By his Excellency

Upon the Petition of Joshua Natstock and Recommendation of many of the Inhabitants of the North part of the Towne of Boston I doe hereby approue of the Said Joshua Natstock to be Master of the Publick Schoole there and to haue and Injoy Such proffits Benefitts and advantages as haue been heretofore payed and allowed to his predecessors—Given under my hand in Boston the four and twentieth day of May, one thousand Six hundred Eighty and Seauen.[32]

This may have been one of the "Two schooles . . . pvided" by the vote of April 30, 1683, a conjecture suggested by the phrases "a free Schoole . . . being now Destitute," and "to haue and Injoy such proffits . . . as haue been heretofore payed and allowed to his predecessors." Such a supposition receives support from a statement of June, 1686, signed by the town treasurer, that "the standinge charge of this town at this time is about 400^{ld}. p.ann—aboue 200^{ld}. of which is in maintaineinge three Free Schools, mending the high wayes in Boston, Rumny Marsh & Muddie riuer."[33]

Only two schools are designated in the town records of the period 1635–1700: the Grammar School, on "School house Street," and the Writing School in Prison Lane. Cotton Mather lamented the fact that there was no school at the North End in 1685 and decided that he would "Never bee at Rest, while our Island here, the North part of Boston is without a good Schoolmaster, and a florishing School."[34] On May 29, 1693, the selectmen "Ordered that Mr Ezekiell Cheever and the other school master shall be paid quarterly."[35] The "other school master" was John Cole, of the Writing School in Prison Lane. Again, a town action, of March 22, 1696/97, refers to "Mr Cole master of the Free writing School of Boston," which implies but one writing school.[36]

If there were "three Free Schools" in 1686, the one not designated

---

[32] *Ibid* (Hutchinson Papers), CCXLII, 342.

[33] B. R., VII, 187.

[34] The Diary of Cotton Mather (*Coll. Mass. Hist. Soc.*, 7th Series, VII, 106), entry of Oct. 24, 1685.

[35] B. R., VII, 215.

[36] B. R., VII, 277.

in the town records became "Destitute" before May 24, 1687, the date of Natstock's appointment. Certainly, Natstock's school ceased to exist when Andros was overthrown, April 18, 1689.[37] Following the governor's departure, the town voted, June 24, 1689, to restore "the former Custome & practice in managing the affaires of the free schools."[38]

It was not until March 11, 1699/1700, that the town voted to establish a writing school at "the North end of Boston," in response to a request from "Some of the Inhabitants" for "the Libertie of a free school, for the Teaching to Write & Cypher."[39] Under the mastership of Richard Henchman, the school was opened, November 1, 1700, probably in a house rented for the purpose.[40] This served until 1718, when the "North Writing School" was erected "at the Charge of" Thomas and Edward Hutchinson, and presented to the town. The new building was on Love Street, on "part of that peice of Land wch the Town formerly purchased of m^rs Susanna Love."[41]

Very likely, the establishment of a writing school at the North End inspired the desire for a grammar school, to complete the educational facilities of that populous part of the town. The earliest known approach to the town on this matter is in a "Proposition for a Free Grãmer School at the North End of Boston. Reced Mar. 10th 1711–12." It follows:

[37] The entry, "John Notstock schoolemaste," in a "Boston Valuation" list of Aug. 27, 1688 (*Mass. Archives*, Usurpation Papers, CXXIX, 139a), indicates that he was teaching at that time. In B. R., I, 135, this entry appears as "John Nontock Schoole maste." On July 11, 1650, "Jo Notstock" signed a certificate, in London, as a Notary Public (*Aspinwall Notarial Records*, 314: an item, in the manuscript volume at the Boston Athenaeum, which has been reproduced accurately in B. R., XXXII, 350).

I have used the initial letter N, because it is unmistakable in four manuscripts. In the petition, it looks like an R, and is so deciphered in the imperfect copy published in *Coll. Mass. Hist. Soc.*, 3rd Series, VII, 186. If the name is of German origin, it should be "Notstock."

[38] B. R., VII, 197. Governor Andros arrived in Boston Dec. 19, 1686.

[39] B. R., VII, 2.

[40] B. R., XI, 4 (Apr. 28, 1701). The town records make no reference to the construction or location of the school.

[41] B. R., VIII, 132 (Mar. 11, 1717/18). The land was "formerly purchased" for the North Grammar School. See also B. R., VIII, 94 (Mar. 9, 1712/13), 101 (Mar. 16, 1713/14), 103 (May 17, 1714), 118–19 (Mar. 12, 1715/16). The North Writing School stood on the southwest side of Love Street, also called Love Lane (now Tileston Street, named after Master John Tileston), between Salem Street and Short Lane (now Wiggin Street).

The Rev. Samuel Mather, who had withdrawn from the Second Church, was permitted "to Preach on the Lords Days at the North Writing School," 1741–42, while the church at the corner of Hanover and Bennet Streets was under construction (B. R., XV, 320, 347–48).

Considerations relating to a free Grañer School in the North Part of Boston

It Cannot but be Thot Strange that One Grammer School Should be Thot sufficient for a Town of above Two Thousand Families when the Law of the Provinces Imposes one upon Every Town that hath above One Hundred.

Education is as great and Good an Interest as can be prossecuted by any People, and the more Liberally it is Prossecuted the more is done for the honour and Welfare of such a People.

The Grañer School in this Town is as full of Scholars as can well Consist with a faithful Discharge of Duty to them.

The North Part of this Town bares no Inconsiderable Share in the Publick Expences and we hope are not altogether unworthy of the Publick benefitts.

It is known that when an hundred and odd Children have been found in the Publick Grañer School not one of that Hundred nor any but the few odd Ones have been Sent from that Part of the Town.

The Distance hath hindred many Parents from Exposing their Tender Children to the Travells of the Winter and the Suñer thither.

Some that Can't be satisfy'd without bestowing a good Cultivation on their Children are at the Charge of a Private Grañer School in the Neighbourhood. Others do Send their Children abroad in the Country.

When the People of that Neighbourhood were Prevail'd withall to Come into the Vote for Additional Incouragements unto the Present Grañer School, they were made to hope that they should ere long be favoured with another Nearer unto themselves.

If the Town will Smile on this just and fair Proposal, it is Probable their will Appear some particular Gentleman whose desire to Serve the Publick will Exert itself on this Occasion and make liberal advances towards the Providing of such Necessary Preliminaries.

These Considerations are humbly offer'd to the Inhabitants of Boston to be Laid in the Ballances of Equity in the Next General Meeting.[42]

On the following day, the town thanked Thomas Hutchinson for offering to build a schoolhouse "at his own Charge," and voted "That there be a Free Grammer School at the North end of this Town."[43] The building, erected on Bennet St. late in 1712, was opened April 20, 1713.[44]

[42] This paper, reproduced in the *New Eng. Hist. Gen. Reg.*, XIII, 260–61, was probably handed to one of the selectmen for consideration at the next town meeting. No signatures are attached to it.

[43] B. R., VIII, 90 (Mar. 11, 1711/12).

[44] B. R., VIII, 91–92 (May 14, 1712). This "peice of Land . . . abt fifty one foot in breadth & abt one hundred feet in length," purchased from Mrs. Susanna Love, extended from Love Street to Bennet Street (now North Bennet Street). The North Grammar School stood on the northeast side of Bennet Street, behind the North Writing School.

On Apr. 29, 1719, the town voted "Thanks . . . unto the donors of the Two North School Houses" (B. R., VIII, 139). See also B. R., XI, 181 (Mar. 23, 1712/13).

Until 1789, when it was discontinued, the school was known as the "North Grammar School."[45]

As early as March 12, 1715/16, the town voted "That a writing School be Erected at the Southerly part of this Town."[46] After a rather leisurely consideration, in town and committee meetings, the town finally voted, December 29, 1718, to proceed with the construction. The building was located "upon ye Comon adjoining to Cowells Lott over agt Mr Wainwrights."[47] Instruction began at the new "South Writing School" shortly after March 15, 1719/20, when the first master was appointed.[48]

According to a town meeting minute of May 17, 1732, the school was "Situated at the uper end of Bond Street in the Souther end of Boston."[49] A visitation report, of June 25, 1740, refers to "the South Writing School in Common Str."[50] The "Propositions for reforming the present System of Public Education in Boston," considered at a meeting of October 16, 1789, place "the School House in West Street."[51] Most of the records, however, use the designation "South Writing School in the Common."[52]

In 1720, the public school system of Boston comprised the South Grammar School, the North Grammar School, the Writing School in Queen Street, the North Writing School, and the South Writing School. No changes were made in this scheme until 1789.[53] Except for the brief period of the British occupation, the schools were in continuous operation from the dates of their establishment.[54]

---

[45] B. R., XXVII, 108 (Dec. 9, 1789): "to be discontinued on Saturday next," Dec. 12. Annexed to the North Writing School.

[46] B. R., VIII, 118.

[47] B. R., VIII, 133–34 (Dec. 29, 1718). See also B. R., VIII, 122 (June 12, 1716), 127 (May 15, 1717), 132 (Mar. 11, 1717/18); XIII, 47 (Dec. 6, 1718). Enlargements were voted in 1744 and 1753 (B. R., XIV, 51, 233).

[48] B. R., VIII, 143.

[49] B. R., XII, 34. See also The Letter-Book of Samuel Sewall, in *Coll. Mass. Hist. Soc.*, 6th Series, II, 134–36. Pond Street is now Bedford Street.

[50] B. R., XV, 246. Common Street is now Tremont Street.

[51] B. R., XXXI, 209. The school stood near the south corner of the present West and Tremont Streets.

[52] The houses on the east side of Common Street were considered "in the Common."

[53] The first committee "to take into consideration the present arrangement of the publick schools in this Town" was appointed Dec. 14, 1781 (B. R., XXVI, 220). It did not complete its work until Oct. 16, 1789 (B. R., XXXI, 208–10).

The schools of Muddy River (Brookline) and Rumney Marsh (Chelsea) have not been included in the study, because the town did not consider them part of its school system.

54 The South Grammar School was closed Apr. 19, 1775 (see p. 4, *supra*). In his "Catalogue of students," Samuel Hunt, master of the North Grammar School, refers to the "cruel Civil War—which drove me from my School at the North Part of the Town, which I left the 6th August," 1775 (Jenks, *op. cit.*, "Catalogue," 107). The writing schools may have closed on Apr. 19, or shortly afterward. On June 5, 1776, the selectmen voted to reopen the South Grammar School, the South Writing School, and the North Writing School (B. R., XXV, 2). The South Writing School was opened July 22, 1776 (B. R., XXV, 3), and the North Grammar School not until Mar. 10, 1779 (B. R., XXVI, 55). On Nov. 8, 1776, the town voted that the "School in Queen Street . . . be immediately opened" (B. R., XVIII, 252).

CHAPTER II

MASTERS AND USHERS OF THE GRAMMAR SCHOOLS

THE FREE SCHOOL, 1635–1684
THE LATIN SCHOOL, 1684–1713
THE SOUTH GRAMMAR SCHOOL, 1713–1775[1]

Philemon Pormort (Master)

"ATT a Generall meeting upon publique notice," April 13, 1635: "Likewise it was then generally agreed upon y[t] o[r] brother Mr Philemon Pormort shalbe intreated to become scholemaster for the teaching and nourtering of children wth us."[2] If he accepted the invitation, he may have remained until 1638, when he removed from Boston to Exeter, New Hampshire.[3]

Daniel Maude (Master)

"At a general meeting of the richer inhabitants," August 12, 1636, Daniel Maude was "chosen" master of the school.[4] He probably continued as master until 1643, when he went to Dover, New Hampshire, as minister.[5]

John Woodbridge (Master)

Probably succeeded Daniel Maude, in 1643. There is but one town record of his connection with the school: "Its ordered that the Con-

[1] I have chosen the first two designations somewhat arbitrarily. See p. 5, *supra*, for names used during the periods indicated.

[2] MS. *Records* . . . 1634–1660 (see p. 1, n. 1, *supra*), and B. R., II, 5.
   Philemon Pormort, b. Grimsby, Lincolnshire, England, s. of Thomas and Dorothy (Dawson) Pormort. Was "under age" when his father's will was proved, Oct. 27, 1603. Married, at Alford, Lincolnshire, Oct. 11, 1627, Susanna, d. of William Bellingham. Left Alford after Nov. 24, 1633. Admitted freeman, Boston, Mass., May 6, 1635 (B. R., XXIX, 136). See also B. R., II, 25, 27, 186, 212; IX, 3, 4, 7, 10, 13, 26, 38, 40, 44, 57; XXXII, 9, 75, 161, 233, 290.

[3] Records of the First Church, "1638, 6th of 11 moneth:" Pormort dismissed with John Wheelwright, with whom he went to Exeter. Later, removed to Wells, Maine. Returned to Boston, and died there between 1653 and 1656.

[4] B. R., II, 160. See also B. R., II, 17, 166, 168, 170, 196, 198 (a deed, of Oct. 8, 1643, mentions "Daniel Maude of Boston"), 209; XXIX, 137 (admitted freeman, Boston, May 25, 1636).
   Daniel Maude, b. 1586, s. of Edward Maude, Master of the Wakefield Grammar School, Yorkshire; B.A., Emmanuel College, Cambridge, 1606/7; M.A., 1610; d. Dover, N. H., 1655.

[5] If Pormort remained in the school until 1638, he probably assisted Maude, as writing master.

stables shall pay unto Deacon Eliot for the use of m[r] Woodbridge eight
pounds due to him for keeping the Schoole the Last yeare," December 2, 1644.[6]

Robert Woodmansey (Master)

Date of appointment unknown. Earliest town record, March 11,
1649/50: "It is alsoe agreed on that M[r]. Woodmansey, the Schoolmaster, shall have fiftye pounds per annum."[7] He may have served until shortly before his death, August 13, 1667.

Daniel Henchman (Usher)

"Agreed with M[r] Danell Hincheman for £40. p. Ann[m] to assisst M[r]
Woodmancy in the grammer Schoole & teach Childere to wright the
Yeare to begine the 1st of March 65–6."[8] Resigned before November 7, 1668, when he was appointed, with three others, to lay out a
town "about twelve miles westward from Marlborough neare the road
to Springfeild."[9] Served again as usher, from March 1, 1669/70 to
March 1, 1670/71.[10]

Benjamin Tompson (Master)

Appointed "schole master," August 26, 1667.[11] At a meeting of the
selectmen, December 29, 1670, "It was agreed and ordered that Mr
Ezechiell Cheeuers should be called to, & installed in the Free Schoole
as head Master thereof, which he beinge then present, accepted of: likewise that M[r] Tompson should be inuited to be an assistant to M[r] Cheeuers in his worke in the schoole, w[ch] M[r] Tompson beinge present, desired time to consider of & to giue his answere;—And, vpon the third
day of January, gaue his answere to Major Generall Leueret in the
negatiue, he haueinge had, & accepted of, a call to Charlestowne."[12]

---

[6] B. R., II, 82.

[7] B. R., II, 99. See also B. R., II, 116 (June 27, 1653), 139 (Aug. 31, 1657), 148
(July 26, 1658); VII, 30 (Mar. 26, 1666).

    Robert Woodmansey, B.A., Magdalene College, Cambridge, 1612/13; M.A., 1616.

[8] B. R., VII, 30.

[9] Recs. of the Gov. and Comp. of the Mass. Bay in New Eng., IV, Pt. ii, 409.

[10] B. R., VII, 63 (Nov. 27, 1671). See also B. R., VII, 57 (Dec. 22, 29, 1670). Cap-
tain in King Philip's War; d. Worcester, Oct. 15, 1685.

[11] B. R., VII, 38.

    Benjamin Tompson, b. July 14, 1642; A.B., Harvard, 1662; A.M.; d. Apr. 13,
1714. Preacher, poet, physician, teacher. See Evans, C., Amer. Bibliog., I, 224, 225,
1376, 1489; and New Eng. Hist. Gen. Reg., XIV, 54, 141; XV, 113, 116. Had taught
at Newtown, L. I., and Westfield, Mass., before coming to Boston.

[12] B. R., VII, 57.

On January 6, 1670/71, he "resigned vp the possestion of the schoole & schoole house."[13]

Ezekiel Cheever (Master)

Appointed, December 29, 1670; received "the key & possession of the schoole . . . as the sole Mast[r] thereof," January 6, 1670/71.[14] Served until his death, August 21, 1708.[15]

Ezekiel Lewis (Usher)

"Psuant to a vote of the Town May 8th [1699] M[r]. Ezekiel Lewis was agreed with and Admitted an Assistant to his Grandfather, Mr Ezekiel Cheever in the Latine free school."[16] Latest record, August 31, 1702.[17] Probably served until Nathaniel Williams was appointed, in 1703.[18]

Nathaniel Williams (Usher and Master)

"The Town by their Vote," June 25, 1703, "do declare their Appro-bation of M[r]. Nathaniel Williams to be an Assistant to m[r]. Ezekiel Chever," and that he "be allowed the Sum of Eighty pounds for the year ensueing in case he accept and perform the aforesaid Service."[19]

[13] B. R., VII, 57. See also Suffolk Deeds, XII, 69; and Coll. Mass. Hist. Soc., 4th Series, VIII, 635. After leaving Boston, he taught at Charlestown, Braintree, and Roxbury.

[14] B. R., VII, 57.
Ezekiel Cheever, b. London, Jan. 25, 1613/14; matriculated at Emmanuel College, Cambridge, Jan. 12, 1632/33, but did not graduate; came to Boston, June, 1637; schoolmaster at New Haven, 1638–50; Ipswich, 1650–61; Charlestown, 1661–71; d. Aug. 21, 1708.

[15] See Hassam, J. T., Ezekiel Cheever and Some of his Descendants, in New Eng. Hist. Gen. Reg., XXXIII, 167–202; and The Diary of Samuel Sewall, in Coll. Mass. Hist. Soc., 5th Series, V, 443; VI, 52, 171, 230–31, 236. Ibid, VI, 231: "Augt. 23, 1708. Mr. Chiever was buried from the School-house. The Gov[r], Councillors, Ministers, Justices, Gentlemen there. Mr. Williams made a handsome Latin Oration in his Honour." See also Evans, op. cit., I, 1384; III, 7870.

[16] B. R., VII, 238 (Aug. 28, 1699). See also B. R., VII, 236 (May 8, 1699). Ezekiel Lewis, b. Nov. 7, 1674; A.B., Harvard, 1695; A.M.; d. Aug. 4, 1755.

[17] B. R., XI, 27.

[18] B. R., VIII, 28 (Apr. 28, 1703): "Voted that the Selectmen do take care to procure Some meet person to be an assistant . . . in the . . . Lattin School." After resigning, Lewis took an active part in town affairs.

[19] B. R., VIII, 29; XI, 33 (May 13, 1703).
Nathaniel Williams, b. Aug. 16, 1675; A.B., Harvard, 1693; A.M.; d. Jan. 10, 1737/38. Prince, T., A Funeral sermon on the Rev. Nathanael Williams . . . (Boston, 1738), 26–27: For a time, missionary in the West Indies, and on his return, private schoolmaster in Boston. His appointment at the public Grammar School did not "hinder him from employing his Intervals of Time, all along, in the Study and Practice of Physick . . . Nor did both these Businesses take off his Heart from the

He "entered upon the Service of the Free School the 12th day of July last," 1703.[20] Upon the death of Ezekiel Cheever, August 21, 1708, he was appointed master; and continued in that position until his resignation, in 1734.[21]

Ebenezer Thayer (Usher)

Probably appointed shortly after December 19, 1709, when the town voted to "defray the Charge of an Assistant" to Nathaniel Williams, until the "Town meeting in march next."[22] At the meeting of March 13, 1709/10, the town instructed the "Inspectors" to agree with "Thayer for his past Service."[23]

Edward Wigglesworth (Usher)

Only town record, June 13, 1715: "Voted. An Addition of Ten pounds p Annum to m^r Wigglesworths Sallery as Usher of the Gramer School."[24]

Benjamin Gibson (Usher)

According to an entry, of March 29, 1720, in Samuel Sewall's diary, "The Inspectors of the Grammar Schools met at the Council Chamber; Sewall, Davenport, Cooke, Savage, and with Mr. Williams the Master, approv'd of Mr. Benjamin Gibson, Bachelour, to be the Usher in School-street."[25] The only town record of his incumbency refers to

---

Ministerial Work . . . And on all Accounts, as a *Scholar, School-Master, Physician, Preacher* and *Christian,* so many Characters united in one Person and in such a Degree, I can't expect to see another like him." See also *Boston Weekly News-Letter,* Jan. 5–12, 1738. Williams was chosen Rector (president) of Yale, but declined the honor. See Dexter, F. B., *Documentary History of Yale University* (New Haven, 1916), 239–40: Letter from N. W., May 13, 1723, to "the Trustees of Yale College"; and *Boston Weekly News-Letter,* Apr. 25–May 2, 1723.

[20] B. R., XI, 36 (Nov. 29, 1703). See also B. R., XI, 34 (July 26, 1703).

[21] B. R., XI, 79 (Sept. 6, 1708); XII, 59–60 (Mar. 12, 1733/34), 86 (May 21, 1734). Opened a private school, after his resignation.

[22] B. R., VIII, 63.

Ebenezer Thayer, b. Feb. 1, 1688/89; A.B., Harvard, 1708; A.M.; d. Mar. 6, 1732/33. Became pastor of the Second Church, Roxbury, Nov. 26, 1712.

[23] B. R., VIII, 66. See Evans, *op. cit.,* I, 2391, 2709, 2967.

[24] B. R., VIII, 113.

Edward Wigglesworth, b. 1693; A.B., Harvard, 1710; A.M.; S.T.D., Edinburgh, 1730; first Hollis Prof. of Divinity, Harvard, 1721–65; Fellow, 1724–65; d. Jan. 16, 1765.

See Evans, *op. cit.,* I, 2594, 3226; II, 3493, 3975, 4209, 4324, 4863; III, 7338, 7592, 8064, 9541.

[25] *Coll. Mass. Hist. Soc.,* 5th Series, VII, 247.

Benjamin Gibson, b. Nov. 4, 1700; A.B., Harvard, 1719; A.M.; d. 1723.

a payment "for his Services as Usher of the Gramer School . . . Ending the Second of May next," 1721.[26] Probably served until July, 1722.[27]

Joseph Green (Usher)

Appointed "Assistant or Usher . . . to Enter upon the Said busynes the Sixteenth of July Current," 1722.[28] Resigned, July 17, 1724.[29]

Samuel Dunbar (Usher)

At a meeting of September 12, 1724, "m[r]. Sam[ll]. Dunbar was approved of by the Select men as Usher to m[r]. Nath[ll]. Williams being Recommended by Him from July 17th. (at which time m[r]. Joseph Green Resigned it)."[30] Probably served until October 17, 1727.[31]

Jeremiah Gridley (Usher)

Appointed "Usher or assistant to m[r] Nathan[ll] Williams at the Gramer School from the 17th octo[r] Instant," 1727.[32] Probably served until February 4, 1733/34.[33]

John Lovell (Usher and Master)

Appears, for the first time in the town records, in connection with a petition, May 10, 1732.[34] Mentioned, July 28, 1732, as "one of the Ushers of the South Gramer School."[35] Probably appointed shortly after March 10, 1728/29, when the town "On the Motion of m[r] Nathan[ll] Williams for another Usher or Assistant . . . Voted That there

[26] B. R., VIII, 152–53 (Mar. 14, 1720/21).

[27] B. R., XIII, 100 (July 14, 1722): The selectmen acted on Nathaniel Williams's "need of An Usher or Assistant in the Gramer School." Gibson had left, or was about to leave.

[28] B. R., XIII, 100 (July 14, 1722).
   Joseph Green, b. June 22, 1701; A.B., Harvard, 1720; A.M.; d. Oct. 4, 1770. See Evans, op. cit., III, 7011.

[29] B. R., XIII, 131 (Sept. 12, 1724).

[30] B. R., XIII, 131.
   Samuel Dunbar, b. May 11, 1704; A.B., Harvard, 1723; A.M.; d. June 15, 1783. See Evans, op. cit., II, 6308, 6309, 6128; III, 6664, 6994, 7185, 8586, 9381.

[31] B. R., XIII, 170 (Oct. 26, 1727).

[32] B. R., XIII, 170.
   Jeremiah Gridley, b. Mar. 10, 1701/2; A.B., Harvard, 1725; A.M.; d. Sept. 10, 1767. Editor, Weekly Rehearsal, 1731–32; Attorney General, Mass., 1767.

[33] B. R., XIII, 248 (Jan. 9, 1733/34); XII, 63 (Mar. 20, 1733/34).

[34] B. R., XII, 31.
   John Lovell, b. Apr. 1, 1710; A.B., Harvard, 1728; A.M.; d. 1778. See Evans, op. cit., II, 5231; III, 7233; IV, 10043.

[35] B. R., XII, 36.

be Alowed the Sum of Eighty Pounds for another Usher of the Said School, when a Sutable Person is Provided to the Satisfaction of the Selectmen as usual."[36] Appointed "Master of the South Grammar School . . . to Succeed the Rev. Mr. Nathanael Williams," May 21, 1734.[37] Left the school, April 19, 1775.[38]

Nathaniel Oliver, Junior (Usher)

Appointed "Usher or Assistant to Mr. Nathanael Williams," January 9, 1733/34, "To Commence from yᵉ 4ᵗʰ. Feb."[39] Resigned, September 10, 1734.[40]

Samuel Gibson (Usher)

Appointed "Usher of the South Grammar School, in the room of mr. Nathanael Oliver . . . to enter into that Service, the 10ᵗʰ. of Septʳ. next, 1734.[41] Last record of incumbency, March 12, 1749/50.[42]

Robert Treat Paine (Usher)

Appointed "usher of said School, to Enter on that Service on Monday next the ninth instant," April, 1750.[43] At a meeting of the selectmen, August 27, 1750, "Mʳ. John Lovell Master of the South Grammar School appeared and informed that Mr. Robert Treat Paine his Usher left that Employment this Day fortnight."[44]

---

[36] B. R., XII, 4. See Jenks, op. cit., "Catalogue," 18n.

[37] B. R., XII, 86. See Boston Weekly News-Letter, May 16–23, 1734.

[38] See Harrison Gray Otis's letter, p. 4, supra. Lovell went to Halifax with the British troops, March, 1776, and died there, 1778.

[39] B. R., XIII, 248; XII, 63 (Mar. 20, 1733/34).
   Nathaniel Oliver, Jr., b. June 2, 1713; A.B., Harvard, 1733; A.M.; d. 1769.

[40] B. R., XIII, 258 (Aug. 14, 1734). See also B. R., XIII, 268 (Mar. 4, 1734/35).

[41] B. R., XIII, 258 (Aug. 14, 1734).
   Samuel Gibson, b. Oct. 31, 1711; A.B., Harvard, 1730; A.M.; d. 1750. Brother of Benjamin Gibson.

[42] B. R., XIV, 239 (Apr. 4, 1750): "Mʳ. John Lovell, master of the South Grammar School appeared and informed the Select men that his late Usher mʳ Samuel Gibson deceᵈ a few days since."

[43] B. R., XVII, 239 (Apr. 4, 1750).
   Robert Treat Paine, b. Mar. 12, 1730/31; A.B., Harvard, 1749; A.M.; LL.D., 1805; d. May 11, 1814. Signer, Declaration of Independence; Attorney General, Mass., 1779–90; Judge, Supreme Court, Mass., 1790–1804.

[44] B. R., XVII, 246.

Nathaniel Gardner (Usher)

Appointed "Usher of the said School," August 27, 1750.[45] Latest town record, May 15, 1759: "Voted that the Sum of Sixty Pounds be allowed and paid to M[r]. Nathaniel Gardner for his Salary as Usher of the South Grammar School."[46]

James Lovell (Usher)

Probably appointed during the illness of Nathaniel Gardner, who died March 26, 1760. Earliest town record, May 16, 1760, "James Lovel ... Usher in the South Grammar School."[47] Left, April 19, 1775, when his father dismissed the school.[48]

THE NORTH GRAMMAR SCHOOL

Recompense Wadsworth (Master)

Appointed, March 30, 1713, to "enter upon the Service of Schoolmaster of y[e] Grammer School at the North on y[e] 20th of Aprill next."[49] Served about two months.

John Barnard (Master)

"M[r] John Barnerd Late of Salem, was by the Sel. men Invited to be y[e] Master of y[e] Gramar School at the North end of Boston in y[e] Room of M[r] R. Wadsworth deceaced ... he being now present doth Signifie his willingness to Accept thereof and to enter upon y[t] Service on the

---

[45] B. R., XVII, 246.

Nathaniel Gardner, b. Oct. 11, 1719; A.B., Harvard, 1739; A.M.; d. Mar. 26, 1760.

[46] B. R., XVI, 24–25. See *Boston Evening Post*, Mar. 31, 1760: "Last Wednesday morning died here, after a very short illness with a Fever, Nathaniel Gardner, jun., M.A. Several Years usher to the South Grammar School in this town."

[47] B. R., XVI, 43.

James Lovell, b. Oct. 31, 1737; son of John Lovell; A.B., Harvard, 1756; A.M.; d. July 14, 1814. See Evans, *op. cit.*, III, 7232, 8640; IV, 12099.

[48] Imprisoned as a spy by British soldiers, June 29, 1775. See the "Diary kept in Boston Goal—Peter Edes—1775" (MS. in Mass. Hist. Soc. library), and "Boyle's Journal of Occurrences in Boston, 1759–1778" (*New Eng. Hist. Gen. Reg.*, LXXXV, 25). Exchanged, Nov. 30, 1776.

Delegate to the Continental Congress; Receiver of Taxes, Collector of the Port, and Naval Officer, at Boston.

[49] B. R., XI, 181. In 1709, he substituted, in the South Grammar School, for Nathaniel Williams, "dureing his present Indisposition" (B. R., XI, 91).

Recompense Wadsworth, b. Mar. 19, 1688/89; A.B., Harvard, 1708; A.M.; d. June 9, 1713. Cotton Mather's treatise, *Golgotha* (Boston, 1713), was occasioned by Wadsworth's death.

27th of August cur[t]."[50] At his own "motion and request," the selectmen voted, January 13, 1718/19, to "dismiss him from the Service of
Schoolmaster."[51]

Peleg Wiswall (Master)

"Invited to take y[e] charge as master of the Free Grāmer School at y[e]
North," April 29, 1719.[52] Accepted, and served until February 9,
1767.[53]

Jonathan Helyer (Usher)

Appointed, September 7, 1738, "Usher of the said School . . . To Commence the 28th of September Currant."[54] At a meeting of the selectmen, January 20, 1741/42, "Mr. Peleg Wiswall Master of the North
Grammar School, Appearing Informed that mr. Jonathan Helyer . . .
hath now resigned."[55]

Samuel White (Usher)

Appointed, January 20, 1741/42, "Usher in the School in the room of
mr. Jon[a]. Helyer."[56] The selectmen reported, May 3, 1745, "that
they Apprehend the Number of Scholars in the North Grammar School
so small as that there is no Occasion for an Usher," whereupon "It was
Voted that the said Usher M[r]. White be Continued in said School until
his next Quarter is compleat and be paid as heretofore, & then be discharged."[57]

Ephraim Langdon (Usher)

Appointed, December 13, 1758. The selectmen "desired that He

50 B. R., XI, 192. Had been master of the grammar school at Salem.
   John Barnard, b. Feb. 26, 1689/90; A.B., Harvard, 1709; A.M.; d. June 14, 1757.
See Evans, op. cit., II, 3390, 4336, 5737.

51 B. R., XIII, 48. Ordained, Apr. 8, 1719; succeeded his father as pastor of North
Parish, Andover, Mass.

52 B. R., VIII, 139.
   Peleg Wiswall, b. Feb. 5, 1682/83; A.B., Harvard, 1702; A.M.; d. Sept. 2, 1767.

53 Resigned on account of illness. See B. R., XX, 243–44 (Feb. 5, 1767): James Lovell
to have "charge of said School," temporarily, beginning Feb. 9, 1767.

54 B. R., XV, 133.
   Jonathan Helyer, b. Apr. 19, 1719; A.B., Harvard, 1738; A.M.; d. May 27, 1745.

55 B. R., XV, 324.

56 B. R., XV, 324.
   Probably one of three Samuel Whites: (1) A.B., Harvard, 1731; A.M.; (2) A.B.,
Harvard, 1740; A.M.; (3) A.B., Harvard, 1741; A.M.

57 B. R., XIV, 73.

would give his Attendance at the School tomorrow," December 14.[58]
Served until August, 1765.[59]

Andrew Eliot, Junior (Usher)

Appointed, January 11, 1765, "to serve the School in that capacity for
one Month," Ephraim Langdon the "Usher . . . being still confined to
his House."[60]

Josiah Langdon (Usher)

Appointed, December 11, 1765, "Usher of the North Grammer School
in the room of Mʳ. Ephraim Langdon deceased."[61] Probably began
teaching early in February, 1765, at the expiration of Andrew Eliot's
"one Month" appointment.[62] Resigned early in 1767.[63]

Samuel Hunt (Master)

Appointed, April 8, 1767.[64] Permitted, October 19, 1768, to "leave
the Charge of the School to his Brother during his absence," in the
country, "which he thought might be a Week."[65] Served until August 6, 1775.[66]

---

[58] B. R., XIX, 100.
  Ephraim Langdon, b. Aug. 7, 1733; A.B., Harvard, 1752; A.M.; d. Nov. 21, 1765.
[59] B. R., XX, 192. See also B. R., XX, 122.
[60] B. R., XX, 127.
  Andrew Eliot, b. Jan. 11, 1743/44; A.B., Harvard, 1762; A.M.; A.M. (Hon.), Yale, 1774; Librarian, Harvard, 1763–67; Tutor, 1767–74; Fellow, 1772–74; d. Oct. 26, 1805.
[61] B. R., XX, 189.
  Josiah Langdon, b. Mar. 3, 1745/46; A.B., Harvard, 1764; A.M.; d. 1779. Cousin of Ephraim Langdon.
[62] B. R., XX, 132 (Feb. 6, 1765): Two of the selectmen were appointed "to treat with Mʳ Josiah Langdon respecting the place of Usher to the North Grammar School, during the confinement of the present Usher."
[63] B. R., XX, 243 (Feb. 5, 1767): "declined officiating any longer." The town clerk wrote "Nathaniel," instead of "Josiah." This is but one of many clerical errors in the town records.
[64] B. R., XX, 249.
  Samuel Hunt, b. Oct., 1745; A.B., Harvard, 1765; A.M.; d. Sept. 8, 1816.
[65] B. R., XX, 313. William Hunt, A.B., Harvard, 1768; A.M.
[66] See p. 11, n. 54. B. R., XXV, 2 (June 5, 1776): Appointed master of the South Grammar School. Served there until 1805.

CHAPTER III

MASTERS AND USHERS OF THE WRITING SCHOOLS

THE WRITING SCHOOL IN QUEEN STREET

John Cole (Master)

APPOINTED, "to keep a Free schoole to teach ye Children of this Towne to read & write for one yeare from the 1st of this instant Nov^r.," 1684.[1] The fact that he received a new appointment, March 10, 1689/90, suggests an interim during which he was not in charge of the school.[2] However, he served from that date until April 12, 1714, when he resigned.[3]

Jacob Sheafe (Master)

Appointed, March 16, 1713/14, "Successor to Mr John Cole," and "entered upon that Service as master of ye Free writing School in Queen Street ye 12th of April cur^t."[4] Served until July 11, 1722, when he became master of the South Writing School.[5]

Edward Mills (Master)

Appointed, July 11, 1722.[6] Probably served until June, 1732, when the town "Voted that m^r Edward Mills School master haue an assistant being in a Bad State of Health."[7]

---

[1] B. R., VII, 171 (Nov. 24, 1684).
John Cole, b. Nov. 17, 1643.

[2] B. R., VII, 200.

[3] B. R., XI, 202 (Apr. 13, 1714). In a letter to the selectmen, Oct. 15, 1713, he says: "I find keeping of the free school grows too hard for me,—and therefore am determined to hold it no longer than this year, which ends in the beginning of the next April, and is the 30th year of my keeping school" (*New Eng. Hist. Gen. Reg.*, XXX, 236).

[4] B. R., VIII, 101; XI, 202 (Apr. 13, 1714).
Jacob Sheafe, b. Feb. 18, 1681/82; d. Dec. 26, 1760.

[5] B. R., XIII, 100. At this meeting of the selectmen, Edward Mills was chosen master of the South Writing School, but the appointment was given to Sheafe, "Signifieing his Desire to take the Charge of the School in the Common, his father's house being near thereto."

[6] B. R., XIII, 100.
Edward Mills, b. June 29, 1665; A.B., Harvard, 1685; A.M.; d. Nov. 7, 1732. Had been master of a private school for many years. See *Mass. Archives*, LVIII, 278; and B. R., XI, 172 (Sept. 8, 1712).

[7] B. R., XII, 36 (June 27, 1732). See also B. R., XIII, 218 (June 14, 1732). Outside of school hours, for some years before his death, he taught "the Children of such in-

Samuel Holyoke (Master)

Appointed, March 13, 1732/33, "master of the School lately kept by Mr Edward Mills Deceaced."[8] Served until early in 1768.[9]

Samuel Holbrook (Master)

Appointed, August 1, 1753, "Writing Master at the School in Queen Street."[10] After this date, there were two masters at the school. Samuel Holyoke was the "Senior Master." According to a town record of August 7, 1754, Holbrook "has resign'd."[11] Probably served until August 9, 1754.

John Proctor, Junior (Master)

Appointed, August 9, 1754, "Writing Master at the School in Queen Street . . . to continue there until next March."[12] Served as "one of the Masters of the Writing School in Queen Street," until late in 1773.[13]

James Carter (Usher and Master)

Appointed, May 4, 1768, "Usher to the Writing School in Queen Street."[14] The "Selectmen desired Him to attend at the School . . . the next Monday being May 9th. 1768."[15] Elected master of the school, November 10, 1773, to begin "on Friday next at 9. o'clock in the Forenoon," November 12.[16] Served until the schools closed, in 1775.[17]

digent Members of the Church of England Gratis, as are not able to pay for the same" (*Boston Weekly News-Letter*, June 21–28, 1733). Appointed by the Society for the Propagation of the Gospel in Foreign Parts.

[8] B. R., XII, 41. Samuel Holyoke, b. Mar. 21, 1694/95; d. Mar. 16, 1768.

[9] Holyoke asked for certain repairs, Sept. 30, 1767 (B. R., XX, 270).

[10] B. R., XVII, 299.
Samuel Holbrook, b. June 26, 1714; A.B., Harvard, 1734; A.M. Had been usher to his brother, Abiah, master of the South Writing School.

[11] B. R., XIV, 261. See also B. R., XIX, 12 (Aug. 15, 1754): Private school license.

[12] B. R., XIX, 12.
John Proctor, Junior, b. Dec. 31, 1726; d. Nov. 4, 1773. Son of John Proctor, former master of the North Writing School. Had been usher at the N. W. S.

[13] B. R., XXIII, 201 (Nov. 10, 1773): "deceased the last Week." "Boyle's Journal of Occurrences in Boston, 1759–1778" (*New Eng. Hist. Gen. Reg.*, LXXXIV, 367), entry of Nov. 4, 1773: "Died Mr. John Proctor, aged 48 years, Master of the Writing School in Queen-Street." See also *ibid*, 265, 267.

[14] B. R., XVI, 247: "has for some Years past been an Assistant to" John Tileston, master of the North Writing School. Had been an apprentice to John Proctor, Jr.
James Carter, d. 1798.

[15] B. R., XX, 291 (May 7, 1768).   [16] B. R., XXIII, 202.

[17] Carter was again master of the school after it was opened by town vote of Nov. 8, 1776 (B. R., XVIII, 252). Appointed, June 5, 1776, "to officiate" as master of the South Writing School, "untill Mr. Holbrook removes to Town" (B. R., XXV, 2).

Abiah Holbrook (Usher)

Appointed, November 10, 1773, on the recommendation of Samuel Holbrook and James Carter.[18] Served until 1775.[19]

THE NORTH WRITING SCHOOL

Richard Henchman (Master)

Appointed, November 1, 1700.[20] Latest town record, March 14, 1714/15.[21] May have served until April 29, 1719.

Jeremiah Condy (Master)

Appointed, April 29, 1719, "master for the New writing School at yᵉ North."[22] Latest town record, December 2, 1730.[23] Probably served until the appointment of John Proctor.

John Proctor (Master)

Appointed, March 9, 1730/31.[24] Served until March 15, 1742/43.[25]

Zachariah Hicks (Usher and Master)

Earliest town record, March 1, 1732/33: "mʳ. Hicks assistant to mʳ. Procter."[26] Probably appointed shortly after June 27, 1732, when the

---

[18] B. R., XXIII, 202.

Abiah Holbrook, son of Elisha Holbrook, was the nephew of Abiah Holbrook (see n. 31, *infra*), and had been one of his pupils at the South Writing School (B. R., XXIX, 318).

[19] B. R., XXV, 78 (Oct. 28, 1778): "entered as Usher under" his uncle, Samuel Holbrook, "Master of the Writing School in the Common," Oct. 26, 1778. Appointed, Nov. 18, 1778 (B. R., XXV, 79); resigned, Nov. 1, 1779 (B. R., XXV, 103).

[20] B. R., XI, 4 (Apr. 28, 1701).

Richard Henchman, b. 1655; d. Feb. 15, 1724/25. Son of Daniel Henchman (p. 13, *supra*). Had been schoolmaster at Yarmouth and Worcester. See The Diary of Samuel Sewall (*Coll. Mass. Hist. Soc.*, 5th Series, VII, 348), entry of Feb. 15, 1724/25.

[21] B. R., VIII, 110. Licensed to sell liquor, July 6, 1719 (B. R., XIII, 55), July 10, 1722 (B. R., XIII, 99), July 8, 1723 (B. R., XIII, 116). See *Acts and Resolves of the Prov. of the Mass. Bay*, X, 291 (June 11, 1723): "A Petition of Richard Henchman, Shewing that for many Years he has taught School in the Town of Boston, but by reason of his Lameness, & advanced age, has been lately render'd Uncapable of that Work, & thereupon has Obtained a Licence for Retailing of Strong Drink."

[22] B. R., VIII, 139.   [23] B. R., XIII, 202.

Jeremiah Condy, b. Jan. 2, 1682/83.

[24] B. R., XII, 21. Had been master of a private school (B. R., XIII, 108).

[25] B. R., XIV, 4.

[26] B. R., XIII, 227.

Zachariah Hicks, bap. Feb. 22, 1701/2; A.B., Harvard, 1724; A.M.; d. July 29, 1761.

town instructed the selectmen to provide an usher for the North Writing School.[27] Left, to become master of the South Writing School, May 13, 1742.[28] Appointed, March 15, 1742/43, "Schoolmaster for the North Writing School in the room of Mr. John Procter who has resigned that place."[29] Resigned in March, 1761.[30]

Abiah Holbrook (Usher)

Appointed, July 19, 1742, " Usher in the said School under mr. Procter, to enter the first of August next."[31] Served until March 23, 1742/43, when he became master of the South Writing School.[32]

John Proctor, Junior (Usher)

Appointed, August 17, 1743, "Usher to m^r. Zech^a. Hicks master of the North Writing School."[33] Served until August 9, 1754, when he became one of the masters of the Writing School in Queen Street.[34]

John Tileston (Usher and Master)

Appointed, August 15, 1754, "Usher at the North Writing School."[35] Succeeded Zachariah Hicks, as master, by town vote, March 23, 1761.[36] "On Wednesday the 2^d. of this Ins^t. April . . . Introduced . . . as Master of that School."[37] Served until the schools closed, in 1775.[38]

James Carter (Usher)

Appointed, April 29, 1761.[39] Served until May 9, 1768, when he became "Usher to the Writing School in Queen Street."[40]

---

[27] B. R., XII, 35–36.

[28] B. R., XII, 297 (May 11, 1742); XV, 344 ("Memorandum" of May 13, 1742).

[29] B. R., XIV, 4.

[30] B. R., XIX, 141 (Mar. 18, 1761): "desired to resign." B. R., XVI, 56 (Mar. 23, 1761): "had resign'd."

[31] B. R., XV, 351.
   Abiah Holbrook, b. July 14, 1718; d. Jan. 28, 1769. After serving an apprenticeship to John Proctor, he had been master of a private school.

[32] B. R., XVII, 10.   [33] B. R., XVII, 28.   [34] B. R., XIX, 12.

[35] B. R., XIX, 13.
   John Tileston, b. Feb. 27, 1735/36; d. Oct. 13, 1826. Had served an apprenticeship to Zachariah Hicks, from 1749 to 1754.

[36] B. R., XVI, 56.   [37] B. R., XIX, 145 (Apr. 15, 1761).

[38] Reappointed, June 5, 1776 (B. R., XXV, 2), and served until 1819. See New Eng. Hist. Gen. Reg., XIX, 342.

[39] B. R., XIX, 147.

[40] B. R., XX, 291 (May 7, 1768). Appointed, May 4, 1768 (B. R., XVI, 247).

William Dall (Usher)

Appointed, May 7, 1768, to "go down to Mʳ. Tilestone's School," May 9, 1768.[41] Latest town record, July 19, 1774.[42] Probably served until the schools closed, in 1775.[43]

THE SOUTH WRITING SCHOOL
Ames Angier (Master)

Appointed, March 15, 1719/20, "School master at yᵉ new writing School House at yᵉ South."[44] Dismissed for incompetence, May 15, 1722.[45]

Jacob Sheafe (Master)

Appointed, July 11, 1722.[46] Latest town record, June 17, 1726.[47] Probably served until May 8, 1727.

Peter Blin (Master)

Appointed, May 8, 1727, "Master of the South School."[48] Latest town record, December 2, 1730.[49] Probably served until March 9, 1730/31.

Samuel Allen (Master)

Appointed, March 9, 1730/31.[50] At a meeting of the selectmen, April 28, 1742, "Mr. Samuel Allen Master of the South Writing School Appeared & Informed that he was very much impaired in his Health and could no longer serve the Town as Master of the said School,

[41] B. R., XX, 291.
  William Dall, b. Dec. 20, 1753; d. 1829. At fifteen, Dall was appointed on an apprenticeship basis.
[42] B. R., XVIII, 181.
[43] B. R., XXV, 46 (Aug. 6, 1777): Reappointed usher in the North Writing School; "Services . . . commenced," June 2, 1777; resigned, Oct. 15, 1777 (B. R., XXV, 50).
[44] B. R., VIII, 143.
  Ames Angier, b. June 29, 1681; A.B., Harvard, 1701; A.M.; d. 1729. Had been master of the town grammar school in Watertown, Mass., and had conducted a private school in Boston (The diary of John Comer, in *Coll. R. I. Hist. Soc.*, VIII, 21). See Evans, *op. cit.*, I, 1661.
[45] B. R., VIII, 164–65.
[46] B. R., XIII, 100.
[47] B. R., XIII, 153.
[48] B. R., VIII, 211.
  Peter Blin, b. Jan. 16, 1703/4.
[49] B. R., XIII, 202.
[50] B. R., XII, 21.
  Samuel Allen, b. Sept. 7, 1706; A.B., Harvard, 1728; A.M.; d. July 21, 1742.

and Desired that some Suitable Person might be Appointed to Supply his place."[51] May have served until May 11, 1742.

Zachariah Hicks (Master)

Appointed, May 11, 1742, and "put . . . into Possession of the South Writing School as Master," May 13, 1742.[52] Served until March 15, 1742/43, when he became master of the North Writing School.[53]

Abiah Holbrook (Master)

Appointed, March 23, 1742/43, "Master of the South Writing School in the room of m^r. Hicks."[54] Served until January, 1769.[55]

Samuel Holbrook (Usher and Master)

Appointed usher, by his brother, Abiah, August, 1745.[56] Resigned, August 1, 1753, to become one of the masters of the Writing School in Queen Street.[57] Appointed master of the South Writing School, March 27, 1769.[58] Served until the schools closed, in 1775.[59]

Joseph Ward (Master)

Was given "Charge of the South Working [sic] School . . . the 28. of January last, and he left it the 10th. of April," 1769.[60]

John Vinal (Usher)

Earliest town record, May 10, 1757: "John Vinal . . . Usher of the Writing School in the Common."[61] His announcement that an evening

---

[51] B. R., XV, 340.

[52] B. R., XII, 297; XV, 344. See also *Boston Weekly News-Letter*, May 6–13, 13–20, 1742.

[53] B. R., XIV, 4.

[54] B. R., XVII, 10.

[55] Died Jan. 28, 1769.

[56] B. R., XIV, 82 (Mar. 11, 1745/46): "Abia Holbrook master of the South Writing School . . . was obliged to appoint his Brother to tend one part of the Scholars . . . Seven months past."

[57] B. R., XVII, 299.

[58] B. R., XXIII, 11. Probably did not begin until Apr. 10, 1769 (see Ward).

[59] B. R., XXV, 2 (June 5, 1776): Appointed master of the South Writing School; B. R., XXV, 111 (Mar. 1, 1780): Resigned.

[60] B. R., XXIII, 21 (June 28, 1769). Appointed, on the death of Abiah Holbrook. "Working" for "Writing" is another clerical error in the town records.

[61] B. R., XIV, 307.

John Vinal, b. Sept. 13, 1724; A.B., Harvard, 1751; A.M.; d. 1823. See Evans, *op. cit.*, VIII, 24962.

school "will be opened the Third Day of October [1756] at the South-Writing-School" indicates that he was an usher there at that time.[62] May have succeeded Samuel Holbrook, August 1, 1753. Served as late as May 15, 1764.[63]

John Fenno (Usher)

Earliest town record, March 9, 1773.[64] Resigned, March 16, 1774.[65]

Andrew Cunningham (Usher)

Appointed, March 16, 1774.[66] Probably served until the schools closed in 1775.

---

[62] *Boston Gazette*, Sept. 13, 27, 1756.

[63] B. R., XVI, 118–19: Has smallpox. Does not appear again in the town records until June 21, 1781 (B. R., XXV, 149), when he was appointed master of the South Writing School. Resigned, June 1, 1795 (B. R., XXXI, 390); ran for governor, received six votes, Apr. 6, 1795 (B. R., XXXI, 392).

[64] B. R., XVIII, 118.

[65] B. R., XXIII, 213.

[66] B. R., XXIII, 213. Had been one of Abiah Holbrook's pupils at the South Writing School (B. R., XXIX, 319).

   Andrew Cunningham, b. Feb. 16, 1760; d. Aug. 29, 1829. At fourteen, he was appointed on an apprenticeship basis.

CHAPTER IV
APPOINTMENTS AND QUALIFICATIONS

THE masters were appointed by the town, or by the selectmen on instructions from the town.[1] Town appointments were made by "Written Votes," in most instances:

According to the Vote of Yesterday the Town proceeded to the Choice of a Schoolmaster for the North Writing School in the room of Mr. John Procter who has resigned that place and upon Collecting and Sorting the Votes it Appeared that Mr. Zechariah Hicks was Chosen by a very great Majority.[2]

When Hicks resigned, John Vinal, usher at the South Writing School, and John Tileston, usher at the North Writing School, petitioned that they "might be appointed to succeed . . . as Master" of the school. "The Town having brought in their Votes, upon sorting them it appeared that the number of Voters were 403, and that M[r]. John Tilestone was chosen Master of the North Writing School by a very great majority."[3]

Often the town authorized the selectmen to make appointments, as in the vote of March 9, 1767:

The Petition of a number of Inhabitants "that a Master may be chosen for the North Grammar School" was read, and debate had thereon, whereupon

Voted, that the Selectmen be a Committee on behalf of the Town to make choice of a Gentleman out of the Candidates that shall offer themselves, as they may most approve of as a Master for said School.[4]

At a meeting, April 8, 1767, "The Selectmen in compliance with the Vote of the Town at their late Meeting respecting the appointment of a Master for the North Grammar School, have unanimously made choice of M[r]. Samuel Hunt Jun[r]. of Cambridge to supply that School."[5] Another illustration of the procedure occurs in a town vote "That the Se-

[1] The first "Inspectors" were requested by the town, Mar. 13, 1709/10, to agree with an usher for the grammar school (B. R., VIII, 66). This did not become the town practice.

[2] B. R., XIV, 4 (Mar. 15, 1742/43). Hicks had been elected master of the South Writing School, May 11, 1742, "by a handy Vote" (B. R., XII, 297). See also B. R., VIII, 29 (June 25, 1703), 139 (Apr. 29, 1719); XII, 86 (May 21, 1734); XXIII, 11 (Mar. 27, 1767). Ushers were usually appointed by the selectmen.

[3] B. R., XVI, 56 (Mar. 23, 1761).

[4] B. R., XVI, 200.

[5] B. R., XX, 249. See also B. R., XVI, 13 (May 16, 1758): "the Selectmen . . . are desired to issue a Warrant for a Town Meeting . . . in Order to know whether the Town will then desire said Selectmen to appoint a Master for the North Grammar School, or an Usher or Assistant to the present Master there."

lectmen take Care to provide a Master for the North Writing School, and make a Return of their doings therein to the next Town Meeting."[6] All emergency appointments were made by the selectmen, without consulting the town. Such actions were reported at subsequent town meetings.[7]

In some cases, the town requested the selectmen to recommend "suitable Persons" for appointment:

The Sel. men pursuant to the Town vote and the directions in the Law have advised ab^t a Master for the Grammer School at ye North, and Accordingly have Treated wth Mr Recompense Wadsworth as judging him to be a Sutable person for that Service, and do accordingly Recomend him to the Town, and do propose that Sixty pounds p. annum be allowed him for ye S^d Service.[8]

Usually, the recommendations of the selectmen were accepted and confirmed by town vote. An interesting instance of "disallowance" appears in connection with the new North Writing School:

Voted. That the Selectmen together with the comittee for Erecting a writeing School House at the North . . . be desired to recomend Some person or persons Sutable for a School-master there, and to make Report thereof to ye Town at their next meeting.[9]

At the "next meeting," the town "Voted a disallowance of the Comittees Report Relating to the Nomination of m^r John Briggs to be master of the New writing School at ye North."[10] The town was not influenced by the presence, on this committee, of Edward and Thomas Hutchinson, the two donors of the school.

The selectmen were enjoined, by the colony law of May 3, 1654, "not to admitt or suffer any such to be contynewed in the office or place of teaching, educating, or instructing of youth or child . . . that haue

---

[6] B. R., XII, 13 (Mar. 10, 1729/30). See also B. R., VII, 236 (May 8, 1699), 238 (Aug. 28, 1699); XIV, 261 (Aug. 7, 1754); XIX, 12 (Aug. 9, 1754).

[7] When Robert Treat Paine resigned unexpectedly, the selectmen appointed Nathaniel Gardner "Usher of said School, until further Orders," Aug. 27, 1750 (B. R., XVII, 246).

[8] B. R., XI, 178 (Feb. 16, 1712/13). Nathaniel Gardner, Junior, "having been recommended to us as a Sutable Person for that trust, and upon Inquiry made into his character," was appointed usher, by the selectmen, Jan. 9, 1733/34 (B. R., XIII, 248). Joseph Green and Samuel Dunbar were recommended by Nathaniel Williams; Robert Treat Paine and Nathaniel Gardner, by John Lovell; Jonathan Helyer, Samuel White, and Ephraim Langdon, by Peleg Wiswall; James Carter, by John Tileston; Abiah Holbrook, by Samuel Holbrook and James Carter; Andrew Cunningham, by Samuel Holbrook.

[9] B. R., VIII, 137 (Mar. 10, 1718/19).

[10] B. R., VIII, 138 (Apr. 29, 1719).

manifested themselves unsound in the faith or scandalous in their liues."[11] According to an enactment of June 28, 1701, grammar school masters had "to be approved by the ministers of the town, and the ministers of the two next adjacent towns, or any two of them, by certificates under their hands."[12] It is probable that similar approval was required for the writing school masters, although they are not mentioned, in this connection, in colony or town actions. In Boston, the town ministers only were consulted:

Whereas the Rev[d] Ministers of this Town have already (most of them) Signified under their hands, their approbation of the Select mens choyce of m[r] Thom[s]. Robie to Succeed as master of the North Grammar School.

Voted. That the Town Clerk be directed in the Name of the Sel. men by the first opportunity to Give the S[d] M[r] Robie an Invitation to under take that charge as master of the S[d] School, and to desire him (as soon as may be) to Signify to them his Mind and Inclination Relating thereto.[13]

Robie delayed so long in making his reply, that the town decided, April 29, 1719, not to "waite any Longer," and voted "That M[r] Peleg Wiswall be by y[e] Select-men Invited to take y[e] charge as master of the Free Grāmer School at y[e] North."[14]

The following action, at a selectmen's meeting, May 14, 1719, indicates that a master might be elected before the approval of the ministers was secured:

Whereas the Inhabitants of this Town at their Last Publick Meeting did make choyce of m[r] Peleg Wiswel to Succeed ⌐⌐ Master of the North Grammer School

Ordered. That the Town Clerk be directed to Notify the R[d] Ministers within the S[d] Town thereof, desireing them to Signifie their Approbation of the S[d] Choyce.[15]

Perhaps the town assumed that the ministers would, as a matter of course, approve a son of the Reverend Ichabod Wiswall.

Newly appointed masters were introduced into their schools by two or more of the selectmen. The town voted, May 11, 1742, that "Mr. Zechariah Hicks shall be Master" of the South Writing School, "and

---

[11] Recs. of the Gov. and Comp. of the Mass. Bay in New Eng., IV, Pt. i, 182–83.

[12] Acts and Resolves of the Prov. of the Mass. Bay, I, 470: "That no minister of any town shall be deemed, held or accepted to be the school-master of such town within the intent of the law."

[13] B. R., XIII, 49 (Feb. 10, 1718/19).

[14] B. R., VIII, 139.

[15] B. R., XIII, 53.

the Select men are desired to Inform him thereof and to Induct him into the Said School."[16] A rather solemn ceremony was used at John Tileston's induction:

On Wednesday the 2ᵈ. of this Insᵗ. April The Selectmen in Body visited the North Writing School, and introduced Mʳ. John Tileston as Master of that School. Their Chairman Mʳ. Cushing in the Name of the whole, inculcated upon the new Master, not only the common and more ordinary dutys of a good Schoolmaster, but also recommended to him such a conduct and be-haviour, as the peculiar Circumstances of his School more especially demanded, and having expressed their hopes that the Just expectation of the Town from his appointment would be answer'd. The Chairman then addressed the Schol-ars, exhorting them to behave with all duty and Respect to their new Master— to improve with diligence and chearfulness, the happy advantages they were under for gaining usefull knowledge; and above all to avoid and shun those Vices and follys which the Youth of the present Day are too prone to indulge themselves in, and to cultivate and practice those Virtues, upon which not only their own happiness, but the future prosperity of the Community so greatly depended.[17]

This is the only introduction of the sort in the town records. Evidently, Thomas Cushing's admonitions to the master and pupils were "espe-cially demanded" by certain "peculiar Circumstances" of the school.

With the exception of Maude, Pormort, Woodbridge, Woodmansey, Henchman, and Cheever, the masters and ushers at the South Gram-mar School were graduates of Harvard College. Maude was a graduate of Emmanuel College; and Woodmansey of Magdalene College, Cam-bridge. The others did not have college degrees. All the masters and ushers at the North Grammar School were Harvard College graduates. At the writing schools, but six masters and three ushers were college graduates, all of Harvard.[18] Those who did not have college degrees were usually men who had had experience as teachers in private schools, or in public schools elsewhere. Three had prepared for teaching by serv-

[16] B. R., XII, 297. See also B. R., XI, 192 (Aug. 18, 1713): Edward Hutchinson and John Ruck were "desired then to Introduce" John Barnard at the North Gram-mar School; XX, 244 (Feb. 15, 1767): Joseph Jackson and Samuel Sewall "should introduce" James Lovell "into said School."

[17] B. R., XIX, 145 (Apr. 15, 1761). Upon resigning from their positions, three of the masters were formally thanked by the town for their "past Services" (B. R., XVI, 56; VIII, 101; XIII, 48). The scarcity of such records suggests that this action may have depended on the esteem in which the masters were held.

[18] Zachariah Hicks counted three times: as usher at the N. W. S., master of the S. W. S., and master of the N. W. S. Samuel Holbrook counted twice: as usher at the S. W. S., and master of the W. S. Q. St.

ing apprenticeships to masters of the town schools.[19] Only one master was dismissed for incompetence; the others seem to have been well qualified for their positions.[20]

Long incumbencies were not unusual. Twelve masters served more than twenty-five years. Peleg Wiswall was master of the North Grammar School for forty-eight years. The record was held by John Tileston, who spent seventy years at the North Writing School: five as apprentice, seven as usher, and fifty-eight as master.

[19] Abiah Holbrook, Jr., to John Proctor; John Tileston, to Zachariah Hicks; and James Carter, to John Proctor, Jr. Many of the masters had "graduated" from the town schools.

[20] After resignation, some became well-known figures in the colony as public officials, preachers, and writers.

CHAPTER V
SUPPORT

"AT a general meeting of the richer inhabitants," August 12, 1636, "there was given" somewhat more than £40 "towards the maintenance of a free schoolmaster for the youth with us."[1] This is the first reference to the support of schools in the records of colonial Boston. Apparently, the town was not ready to bear the entire expense of establishing a free school. On this occasion, some of the wealthier, public-spirited citizens decided to encourage the town in connection with the plans which had been made in the preceding year.[2] The support of the school for at least one year was assured by this donation. Records of later date indicate that the school was in continuous operation from this time until April 19, 1775.

According to John Winthrop, Boston, during the period 1630–1649, "made an order to allow forever 50 pounds to the master and a house, and 30 pounds to an usher . . . and the charge to be by yearly contribution, either by voluntary allowance, or by rate of such as refused."[3] There is no reference to this action in the town records, and nowhere, throughout the seventeenth and eighteenth centuries, do they mention any kind of "yearly contribution, either by voluntary allowance, or by rate of such as refused." Furthermore, *The Records of the Governor and Company of the Massachusetts Bay* do not mention a Boston "order" of the sort, which Winthrop says "was confirmed by the general court."[4] Such a practice may have been considered at the meeting of August 12, 1636, at which Winthrop was present, but it was not established.

The first General Court enactment on the subject, 1647, required "that every township in this jurisdiction after the Lord hath increased them to the number of fifty house holders, shall then forthwith appoint one within their town to teach all such children as shall resort to him to write and read, whose wages shall be paid either by the parents or masters of such children, or by the inhabitants in general by way of

---

[1] B. R., II, 160. Because of omissions from the record, the exact sum cannot be determined. The largest contributions were from the Governor, and the Deputy Governor.

[2] Philemon Pormort had been invited to become schoolmaster, Apr. 13, 1635 (B. R., II, 5).

[3] Winthrop, John, *The History of New England from 1630 to 1649* (2 vols. Ed. by James Savage. Boston, 1853), II, 264.

[4] Ed. by N. B. Shurtleff. 5 vols. in 6. Boston, 1853–54.

supply, as the major part of those who order the prudentials of the town shall appoint . . . and . . . where any town shall increase to the number of 100 families or householders, they shall set up a grammar school."[5] Each town in the colony was permitted to "appoint" its own method of supporting public schools.

When the town of Boston first considered a method of support, at a general meeting of *all* the inhabitants, it "Ordered," January 10, 1641/42, "that Deare-Island shall be Improoved for the maintenance of a Free schoole for the Towne, and such other Occasions as the Townsmen For the time being shall thinke meet, the sayd schoole being sufficiently Provided for."[6] It was not until December 30, 1644, that Deer Island was leased, "unto James Penn, and John Oliver for these three years next ensuing paying unto the Use of the Schoole seaven pounds per yeare."[7] At the expiration of this period, it was "lett to Edward Bendall, January 31, 1647/48, "for the tearme of seaven years . . . he . . . to pay to the Towne of Boston the sum of fourteen pounds per annum for the scooles use of the sayd Towne in provision and clothing."[8]

On March 12, 1648/49, the selectmen were instructed to "take order aboute Long Iland and Spectacle Iland, with them that now hold it, to instate it on them for Inheritance, upon paying a yearly rent upon evrye accre for the Schols use."[9] By agreements, of April 9, 1649, the land on these islands was leased for "six pence an accre per year . . . for the use of the schole."[10]

The town hoped to find, in the three islands, a dependable source of income. Within a few years, however, the lessees were in default. At a

[5] *Recs. of the Gov. and Comp. of the Mass. Bay in New England*, II, 203 (Nov. 11, 1647).

[6] B. R., II, 65. On Mar. 4, 1634/35, the General Court granted "Deere Iland, Hogg Iland, Long Iland, & Spectakle Ileland . . . to the inhabitants of Boston . . . payeing to the Tresurer . . . the yearely rent of iiij^s" (*Recs. of the Gov. and Comp. of the Mass. Bay in New England*, I, 139).

[7] B. R., II, 82. See also B. R., II, 98 (Nov. 31, 1649); VII, 174 (Mar. 4, 1684/85).

[8] B. R., II, 92. The period was "made up twenty and one years," Feb. 26, 1648/49 (B. R., II, 93). See also B. R., II, 97 (June 26, 1649): "for the schols use," land in Bendall's Cove leased for £3/2/2; and a "parcill of land by his house" leased to Benjamin Ward for £3 per annum. B. R., VII, 14 (Feb. 23, 1662/63): Deer Island assigned for thirty-one years, "att £14 rent to be payed yearly . . . for the use of the Free Schoole."

[9] B. R., II, 94.

[10] B. R., II, 95. See also B. R., II, 140 (Nov. 30, 1657): "two acres" on Long Island "lett to Wm. Wimburne for ever, paying a bushel of merchantable barly malt yearely to the Schooles use," from Mar. 1, 1657/58.

meeting of the selectmen, April 27, 1655, the constable was ordered to "distrayne upon Deare Island for the rent that is due."[11] In the case of Long Island and Spectacle Island, "a considerable part of the rent due to the use of the schoole" was "Nott brought in," and it was "therefore ordered that the present renters shall within ten dayes after the date hereof," June 25, 1655, "come in and cleare their severall payments due for said land, upon forfeiture of said lands as by former agreement."[12]

Long Island and Spectacle Island are not mentioned, in the records, as sources of income after March 11, 1666/67, when the town voted that the "annuall rent" from these islands "is made voyde."[13] Although Deer Island continued to be leased, the school was not designated as the beneficiary of the income after May 25, 1685.[14]

A town meeting record of March 11, 1649/50 refers to "the 2000 acers" at Braintree, which were "set apart for the schools use."[15] Moses Paine "hath let to him 500 accers of land to be layd out at Braintry, painge forty shillings per annum for ever, for the schols use . . . in corne or porke at the prize curant . . . to be payd into the towne treasuree."[16]

"In ans^r to the petition of the toune of Boston," the General Court voted, October 16, 1660, "to graunt . . . one thousand acres of land, for their furtherance & helpe to dischardg ye chardg of a free schoole."[17] There seems to have been no pressing need of the grant, for it was not until April 25, 1664, that the selectmen instructed one of their number "to looke after the layeing out the 1000 Ackers of land for the vse of the Free Schole."[18] The General Court located the tract "in the wilderness on the North of the merimack River."[19] Nothing was done about the matter until January 1, 1701/2, when the town clerk was asked to "procure a record out of the Secretaryes office of the Gen^{ll} Courts grant."[20] The "record" was then filed, and forgotten. Twelve years later, one of the selectmen was "desired to Imploy one or more meet persons to find out the thousand Acres of Land on the North Side of Merimack a River, formerly granted by ye Gen^{ll} Court to this Town wth Reffer-

[11] B. R., II, 125.   [12] B. R., II, 125.   [13] B. R., VII, 34.
[14] B. R., VII, 177; XI, 149–50, 152; VIII, 121; XIII, 48, 144, 146, 225; XIV, 236; XIX, 154; XX, 214; XVI, 220, 237–38; XXIII, 168.
[15] B. R., II, 99. There is no earlier record of this action.
[16] B. R., II, 95 (Apr. 19, 1649): "9:2:mo," in the records, should be "19:2:mo." See minutes of Feb. 25, 1666 (B. R., VII, 33).
[17] Recs. of the Gov. and Comp. of the Mass. Bay in New England, IV, Pt. i, 444.
[18] B. R., VII, 22.
[19] Mass. Archives, LVIII, 53 (May 13, 1664; Oct. 19, 1665).   [20] B. R., XI, 14.

ence to ye Free School and to make return to the Sel. men in order that they may know where to find the Same hereafter."[21] On December 3, 1720, the selectmen voted to employ two surveyors "to renew the bounds of ye Farm granted to the Free-School ... the Auntient boundaryes being now difficult to be found."[22] After May 21, 1735, the grant disappears from the records, leaving no trace of income for the school.[23]

Various parcels of land within the town were rented or sold "for the schooles use."[24] Occasionally, the town received a legacy of land or money for this purpose.[25] "Itt is ordered that the ten pounds left by legacy to the use of the school in Boston by mis. Hudson, deceased, shall bee lett to Capt. James Olliver for sixteen shillings per annum, so long as he pleases to improve itt."[26]

Town and selectmen's minutes indicate that the sources of income for the support of the school, during the seventeenth century, were the donations of August 12, 1636, Deer Island, Long Island, Spectacle Island, the land at Braintree, land in town for building and dock purposes, and legacies of land and money.[27] In addition, there was the town treasury in which all moneys were deposited.

[21] B. R., XI, 208 (June 14, 1714). The town did not move to engage a surveyor, until Apr. 17, 1716 (B. R., XIII, 3).

[22] B. R., XIII, 77. This vote was repeated, Feb. 20, 1720/21 (B. R., XIII, 79).

[23] B. R., XII, 110: "The Committee have also obtained Copys of the Grant." Another grant, requested at this meeting, and secured Dec. 29, 1735 (B. R., XII, 124), was later sold for £3660 (B. R., XII, 179), but the money was used for repairing the town batteries.

[24] B. R., II, 123–24 (Mar. 30, 1655), 126 (July 30, 1655), 130 (Mar. 31, 1656), 133 (Feb. 23, 1656/57); VII, 38 (Oct. 28, 1667), 150–52 (Jan. 30, 1681/82): Indenture of sale, Oct. 20, 1669, recorded. Other rents (1646–1685) for the "free Schoole" are indicated in *Suffolk Deeds*, I, 115–16; II, 121, 259; III, 454; IV, 256, 294; V, 395; VII, 170, 292; VIII, 450; IX, 284, 286, 317; XII, 215; XIII, 174, 497; XIV, 135.

[25] The "land that Christopher Stanley gave in his will for the schols use," mentioned in the town records, Apr. 19, 1649 (B. R., II, 95), was "a pcell ... lying neere to the water side & four rodds in length backward" (*Suffolk County Probate Records*, I, 57). See also John Cotton's will, Nov. 30, 1652: One half of his "ffarme & grounds at Muddy River" to the "free Schoole in Boston" (*Suffolk County Probate Records*, I, 73).

[26] B. R., II, 124 (Mar. 30, 1655). Will of Mrs. Mary Hudson, Sept. 26, 1651 (*Suffolk County Probate Records*, I, 60–61). Robert Keayne, who died Mar. 23, 1655/56, bequeathed "fivety pounds ... to the use of the free school at Boston" (*Suffolk County Probate Records*, I, 167).

[27] As indicated above, the General Court grant of 1000 acres was unproductive. In 1710, Samuel Sewall thought that the first free school had been well taken care of "by a Town not eighty years old" (Letter to Increase Mather, Apr. 25, 1710, in *Coll. Mass. Hist. Soc.*, 6th Series, I, 391).

With the establishment of new schools, the town adopted the practice of assigning specified incomes for their support. When "the wast Lands at Brantree," were sold, the town voted, January 24, 1708/9, "that the income of the five hundred pounds be forever impropriated and improved for a School or Schools for writing and Arithmetick."[28] Another grant to the writing schools was made, March 10, 1711/12: "The Sume of one hundred ninety two pounds eight Shill. & Six pence money recd for the Land at Brooklyn . . . the money to be Applyed to the Same use that the five hundred pounds for the Land at Brantree is appropriated."[29]

The remainder of the "Towns Land at Brantry" was sold in 1711, and £1300, "part of the Purchase money," was set aside for investment "in Some Real Estate for the use of the Publick Lattin School."[30] A marsh was "Granted to" Col. Joshua Lamb, April 27, 1720, "upon his paying into the Town Treasury . . . the Sume of Seventy pounds. And the Sd money to be invested in Some Real Estate, for the use of the First Free Gramer School in Boston."[31]

At a meeting of May 9, 1711, the town "Voted. That it be left wth the Selectmen to draw up & Offer to the Town Such proposalls as they Shall thinck proper, in order to an appropriation of the Townes Wharfe & Dock at Merryes point, ye Rent of Winimisit Ferry & the Wharfe at ye end of Cross Street, For the Support of a Free School or Schools at the North end of the Town."[32] A vote of March 11, 1711/12 appropriated "the Townes Wharfe, Dock and Flatts at the North Battree . . . towards the Support of the Free Grammar School at the North end of Boston."[33] The town, at this time, was considering the establishment of another grammar school.

When it was decided, March 13, 1715/16, "That a writeing School be erected at the Southerly part of this Town," the "United Committee who have money to lay out" was "desired to apply the Same, for such a

[28] B. R., VIII, 56. See also B. R., VIII, 73.

[29] B. R., VIII, 90.

[30] B. R., VIII, 77 (Mar. 13, 1710/11), 81 (May 9, 1711). On the latter date, Samuel Sewall was released from "an Annual Quit claim of Forty Shillings. Issueing out of a Ceader Swamp . . . in Brooklyne, Appropriated to the use of the Grammar School," in consideration of an abatement of £70 on a sale of land to the town. The £70 were to be invested for "the use of the Free Grammar School."

[31] B. R., VIII, 146.

[32] B. R., VIII, 81. The wharf and dock at Merry's Point were leased for £10.

[33] B. R., VIII, 90.

School."[34] In 1721, Samuel Sewall gave, "for the Use of" the South Writing School, an "Annuity of yearly Rent of Five pounds four shillings . . . out of a certain piece or parcel of his Pasture-Land called Elm Pasture."[35] After Sewall's death, his heirs were released from the "Annuity . . . Charged on . . . Elme Pasture . . . upon their Paying the Sum of One Hundred Pounds . . . Which Sum is Hereby Appropriated and Sett apart for ever to be let to Intrest . . . for the use and Benefit of the School."[36]

For "the Support of the Writing Schools," the town instructed a committee, March 9, 1724/25, "to Erect a building . . . The Income and Rent thereof to be paid into the Town Treasury Annually."[37] The "Warehouse opposite the Golden Ball . . . was a Donation to the Town and the Income appropriated for the Maintenance and support of the Publick Schools."[38]

Boston shared, also, in certain fines that were provided by General Court enactment. A law, passed June 29, 1700, required that all who sold "wine, brandy, rhum, or other distilled liquors, beer, ale, perry, or cyder, by retail, without having licence . . . shall forfeit and pay the sum of four pounds, one-half thereof to the informer, and the other half to and for the use and support of a free grammar- or writing school or schools in the town where the offence shall be committed."[39] Those who failed "to give a true list of their estate and polls" were subject to a fine of forty shillings, one "half to be paid for and towards the support of the schoolmaster in said town."[40]

The brief treatment in the preceding pages includes every recorded town and colony action on the support of schools in colonial Boston. Because of the incompleteness of the records, it is impossible to estimate, for any particular year, the sum of money available, from all sources, for the use of the schools. In case of deficiency, the town had recourse to its treasury, or to a "rate" which included the school among other "necessary Charges." Postponement of payments for salaries and for repairs of school buildings was not unknown, but eventually these obligations were met.

---

[34] B. R., VIII, 118. See also B. R., X, 86 (June 17, 1717).

[35] The Letter-Book of Samuel Sewall (*Coll. Mass. Hist. Soc.*, 6th Series, II, 134–36).

[36] B. R., XII, 34 (May 17, 1732).   [37] B. R., VIII, 189.

[38] B. R., XVI, 144–45 (May 14, 1765).

[39] *Recs. of the Gov. and Comp. of the Mass. Bay*, I, 435, 477 (June 18, 1701), 529 (July 31, 1703).

[40] *Ibid*, I, 516 (Mar. 17, 1702/3).

At no time during the colonial period was there a special tax in Boston for school purposes only. It was necessary, occasionally, to raise money for the maintenance of the schools; but, in every instance, these institutions were listed with other town charges. The practice is sufficiently illustrated by the action of a town meeting, September 18, 1699: "It was then voted that the Selectmen should raise a Tax on the inhabitants of s^d. town to the value of £800 for the relief of the poor, for the payment of Schoolmasters & payment for repairing of the Town house and all other necessary Charges arising w^thin s^d. town."[41]

In the town meeting minutes of March 12, 1710/11, the statement, "the Free School is maintained cheifly by a Town Rate on the Inhabitants," should not be misinterpreted. It refers to the general tax, not to a special levy for the school.[42] When Samuel Sewall gave an annuity of £5/4/0 to the South Writing School in 1721, he said, in his deed, that it was for the purpose of "lessening the Town-Tax made for the payment of Salaries of Writing Schoolmasters."[43] He referred not to a tax levied for that particular charge, but merely to that part of the general tax receipts which was used for the writing schools. Each of the three writing school masters received £100, in 1721. It may be of interest to note that the general "grants," or taxes, to be "Raised on the Inhabitants & Residents of this Town for defraying the Necessary Charges," in 1719, 1720, 1721, and 1722, were £1800, £2000, £2700, and £2500.[44]

At a meeting of March 11, 1750/51, "The Petition of several Inhabitants praying the Town would Consider of the great Expence occasion'd by the Publick Schools, and determine whether one Grammar School, and two Writing Schools are not sufficient for the Education of the Children of the Town.—was Read."[45] Although the "said Petition was withdrawn," a committee was appointed "to make a full and particular Enquiry into the present State of the Town, and what are the Causes of the great Expence thereof, and Consider what Method the Town can take in order to prevent or reduce the same."[46] The schools were considered in the first section of the committee's report:

[41] B. R., VII, 238. See also B. R., VII, 187 (May 14, 1686); VIII, 3 (Mar. 11, 1699/1700), 7–8 (May 12, 1701).
[42] B. R., VIII, 78.
[43] See note 35.
[44] B. R., VIII, 138, 145, 154, 166.
[45] B. R., XIV, 187–88.
[46] B. R., XIV, 192 (Mar. 12, 1750/51).

That the Charge of supporting the several Publick Schools amounted the last Year to more than ⅓ part of the whole Sum drawn for by the Selectmen; but altho this Charge is very Considerable, & the number of Schools is greater than the Law requires, Yet as the Education of Children is of the greatest Importance to the Community; the Committee cannot be of Opinion that any Saving can be made to Advantage on that head; except the Town should think it expedient to come into Methods to oblige such of the Inhabitants who send their Children to the Publick Schools and are able to Pay for their Education themselves, to ease the Town of that Charge by assessing some reasonable Sum upon them for that purpose.

After this "Paragraph was Debated, and the following Question put Viz^t. Whether the Town will come into any Alteration or other method than they now have relating to the Schools," the town "Voted in the Negative, & that that Paragraph of said Report be not Accepted."[47] The general tax voted in 1750, and 1751, was £4000 "lawful money" in each year.[48] The salaries of schoolmasters and ushers amounted to £670, in 1751.

The schools established by the town of Boston were "public schools," open to all. They were also "free schools," in which no tuition-fees were imposed upon residents of the town.[49] Non-residents were obliged to pay for the instruction of their children:

Whereas the Support of the Free Schools of this Town hath been, and still is, at ye Cost & charge of the Inhabitants of ye Said Town and the Select men being informed of Several Instances, of Children Sent to ye S^d Schools, whose parents, or others who of Right ought to defray the Charge of their Education, do belong to other Townes or Precincts.

Where fore they ye S^d Select men do direct the S^d School masters to demand & receive of the persons Sending any Such children the accustomed recompence for their Schooling, and to Return unto ye Select men a List of their names, once (at ye Least) every year.[50]

In addition to the "accustomed recompence," there were fees for "en-

---

[47] B. R., XIV, 197–98 (May 14, 1751).

[48] B. R., XIV, 177 (May 15, 1750), 197 (May 14, 1751).

[49] When the selectmen decided, Apr. 30, 1683, to "pvide" two writing schools, it was "agreed . . . y^t such psons as send theire children to schoole (y^t are able) should pay something to ye Master for his better incouragement in his worke" (B. R., VII, 158, 161). It was found, however, that the master's salary could be increased; and the suggestion was not put into practice (B. R., VII, 171).

[50] B. R., XI, 137 (June 18, 1711). In all cases, whether of non-residents, or of those who had just removed to Boston, applications for admittance had to be submitted to the selectmen for approval. See B. R., XV, 225 (Feb. 27, 1739/40); XIX, 240 (Dec. 15, 1762), 295 (Dec. 29, 1763).

trance" and "firing" which were paid by non-resident pupils. On April 2, 1725, Samuel Sewall "paid Entrance-Money 5ˢ," at the Writing School in Queen Street, for his nephew, Benjamin Sweet, who had come from Newbury to live with him. He paid five shillings "To Mr Sheaf for Fuel," September 29, 1725.[51]

A small fee for fire-wood, called "firing," or "fire-money," was expected of residents whose "circumstances" permitted.[52] It was not demanded by town regulation, however. In Ezekiel Cheever's day, it was six shillings.[53] Entrance fees were not required of resident pupils, although some of the masters regarded such charges as their perquisites. After an "enquiry into the Circumstances of the North Writing School," in 1741, the selectmen reported to the town that no "Children of the Town have been refused, that could Read in the Psalter, nor any Demand of Entrance Money made of the Inhabitants, but only from Strangers Children, of which there is now about Ten in the School, and that for Firing some that are in low Circumstances Pay Nothing, others as they think fit, so that One with Another, it Amounts to about Five Shillings a peice, the which Perquisites the Master insists on as his right and without it, can't Subsist in keeping the School."[54] Ten years later, the town "Voted that the several Masters of the Publick Grammar Schools and Writing Schools in the Town be directed not to refuse taking into their respective Schools, any Child or Children that may be brought to 'em for Education, in case Enterance money (so called) is not paid said Masters, and also that they shall not demand any Pay or Allowance for Instructing such Children, as belong to the Town, and that attend in School hours only . . . Also Voted that the Selectmen . . . give Directions to said Masters what money they may receive from the Scholars, for defreying the Expence of Firing."[55] The town records do

---

[51] Both records are in Samuel Sewall's ledger (MS. at the New Eng. Hist. Gen. Soc.), fol. 178.

[52] B. R., XIV, 162 (May 9, 1749): "the Selectmen are desired to provide suitable Books for" reading and spelling, "at the Charge of the Town, to be given to such Poor Children as they may think proper."

[53] The "Accompt of Martha Balston late Ballard," Apr. 27 1716 (*Suffolk County Probate Records*, XIX, 253): "To Cash pᵈ. Mʳ. Cheivers for 7 years firing him [Robert Ballard, her son] at 6ˢ . . . . . . 2 . . 2 . . "

[54] B. R., XII, 279 (May 8, 1741). See also B. R., XV, 288 (Apr. 15, 1741).

[55] B. R., XIV, 199 (May 14, 1751). See also B. R., XXXI, 18 (Apr. 5, 1784): "Voted that the practice of Schoolmasters in receiving Entrance & Fire Money (so called) be abolished as inconsistent with that Freedom of Education which was originally intended in the Institution of the Publick Schools."

not indicate the amounts of the fees for entrance, or for the tuition of non-residents.

The schools were designed to be free of charges to the residents of Boston. "Our free schools seem to have been interested for the Benefit of the Poor and the Rich; that the Children of all, partaking of equal Advantages and being placed upon an equal Footing, no Distinction might be made among them in the Schools on account of the different Circumstances of their Parents, but that the Capacity & natural Genius of each might be cultivated & improved for the future Benefit of the whole Community."[56]

[56] B. R., XXXI, 16: A town committee report, Apr. 5, 1784.

CHAPTER VI

SALARIES AND ALLOWANCES

AS a rule, the salaries of the masters and ushers were paid from the town treasury. "Voted that m^r Benjamin Gibson be allowed & paid out of the Treasury the Sum of fifty pounds for his Services as Usher."[1] In a few instances, money owing to the town was paid directly to the masters, and not to the treasurer. Robert Woodmansey, in 1657, was "alowed to have the rent [£2] due from Leiut. Richard Cook for these two yeares past."[2] At a meeting of May 29, 1693, it was "Ordered that Mr Ezekiel Cheever and the other school master shall be paid quarterly and that orders be passed to the Treasurer for it. Mr Cheever salery to be sixty pounds in mony and that Mr Nathaneel Oliver bee discharged from all former dues for the Marish hired of the Town upon his payment of the present quarters rent to Mr Cheever."[3]

In 1684, John Cole "agreed . . . to keepe a Free schoole to teach ye children of the Towne to read & write for one yeare . . . for which the Towne is to pay him 10^{ld}. in mony & 20^{ld}. in Countrie pay as mony, or at mony price."[4] This is the only town record of payment to a schoolmaster of Boston, in provisions, or other commodities. Ezekiel Cheever's salary, in 1693, was "to be sixty pounds in mony." After this date, sums of money are indicated in all records of salary payments.

In most cases, salaries were determined and voted in town meetings. The records of the period 1635–1775 indicate the amounts of some three hundred and nine salary awards to masters and ushers. Of these, but thirty-three were voted by the selectmen. From 1644 (the year of the first salary record) to 1700, there were six salary actions by the selectmen, and two by the town; from 1701 to 1713, seventeen by the selectmen, and five by the town; from 1714 to 1774, ten by the selectmen, and two hundred and sixty-nine by the town. Before 1750, most of the salary awards were determined at the town meeting in March; after that date, in May.[5]

---

[1] B. R., VIII, 152–53 (Mar. 14, 1720/21).

[2] B. R., II, 139 (Aug. 31, 1657). See also B. R., II, 109 (Mar. 29, 1652), 117 (Aug. 28, 1653).

[3] B. R., VII, 215. This marsh had not been designated as a source of support for the school.

[4] B. R., VII, 171 (Nov. 24, 1684).

[5] Of two hundred and eight awards during the period 1750–1774, only twenty-two

Before 1713, the selectmen appear to have acted largely on their own authority in awarding salaries. In all cases, however, including those in which definite orders were not given them, the authority which they exercised was conferred upon them by the town. Occasionally, in that early day, they received specific instructions from the town. "At a public meeting of the inhabitants of Boston," March 13, 1698/99, it was "Voted, That an Assistant be Provided to be wth Mr. Cheever, in the Latine School," and that it "be left to the Selectmen, to make Choice of the pson, and to Treat wth him about his Sallary, making report thereof to the Town."[6] In May, the town voted "That the Selectmen shall agree wth Mr Ezekiel Lewis, for his Salary as an Assistant to . . . Mr Ezekiel Cheever in the Latine School, not exceeding 40^ld. p. year."[7] The final memorandum on the matter is contained in the selectmen's minutes of August 28, 1699: "Psuant to a vote of the Town May 8th. M^r. Ezekiel Lewis was agreed with and Admitted an Assistant to his Grandfather, Mr Ezekiel Cheever in the Latine free school, his salary at psent to be 40^ld. p. year."[8] After 1713, the sums designated by the selectmen were those which were customarily assigned by the town, and most of these were awarded in connection with emergency appointments.

The town did not establish a "pay day," on which all schoolmasters received their stipends. Each salary was "to be paid quarterly as it shall become due."[9] The quarters began with the dates of appointment. This good intention was not always carried out, however. Salary payments were often in arrears. A full year's salary was owing to Daniel Henchman after he left the "free Schoole."[10] In a petition of 1687, or 1688, addressed to Governor Andros, Ezekiel Cheever remarked that "there is due to me about fifty five pounds for my labours past."[11] At that time, his salary was £60 per year. Not long afterward, the selectmen "Ordered y^t Capt Townsend pay Mr Ezechiell Cheev^rs 10^ld. pte of Areeres due to him From the Towne."[12] Cheever's usher, Ezekiel Lewis, appointed

were not fixed in May; and, of the latter, seven were determined Mar. 10, 1751/52, and eight on July 19, 1774. The other seven attached to emergencies.

6 B. R., VII, 234.   7 B. R., VII, 236.

8 B. R., VII, 238. See also B. R., VII, 158 (Dec. 18, 1682), 161 (Apr. 30, 1683), 171 (Nov. 24, 1684), 227 (Mar. 22, 1696/97).

9 This phrase occurs in most of the records of salary actions.

10 B. R., VII, 63 (Nov. 27, 1671).

11 *Mass. Archives* (Hutchinson Papers), CCXLII, 343.

12 B. R., VII, 201 (Mar. 11, 1689/90).

August 28, 1699, was awarded, March 2, 1701/2, "£11.5.0. for his q^r Sallery to ye 28th of Feb^{ry} last."[13] His next payment was awarded six months later.[14]

At times, the town considered other obligations more pressing, and gave them precedence. This practice, repeated throughout the years, inspired many petitions from the masters. In 1705, the town treasurer was instructed to "take care for the payment of the Severall School-masters out of the first money he can procure."[15] As late as 1776, a committee appointed "to examine the State of the Town Treasury," asked "whether it would not be best, in future, that the Money granted for each particular Year, should be invariably applied to defray the Expenses of that year only, & that it be made a Rule, that the first Draughts should be paid first." The committee expressed the "Opinion, that a Regulation of this kind, would be for the Credit of the Town, & encourage the Hearts of the Officers of the Town, as every Man [would] then be assured of his Money in his Turn, without any needless Attendance, & the Punctuality would prevent those *useful* Servants of the Town, the *Schoolmasters*, from appearing, by their Heirs, as Creditors of the Town."[16]

Of particular interest, at this point, are the minutes of a "Meeting of the Freeholders and other inhabitants," May 11, 1762:

The Petition of a number of the Masters of the Town Schools, setting forth, that they meet with great difficultys in obtaining payment of the several Salaries which the Town has been pleased to assign them—that notwithstanding a Vote formerly passed for their payment Quarterly, they having been to their great distress kept out of their pay from Year to Year, and for what they do receive at any time are obliged to the friendship of particular Gentlemen, who by the kind permission of the Collectors, are willing to pay their Taxes into their hands, that your Petitioners have some of them nine some twelve and some eighteen Months Salary due to them—that they are informed that the

13 B. R., VII, 238; XI, 17.

14 B. R., XI, 27 (Aug. 31, 1702): "Ezekiel Lewis is allowed £22.10s for his halfe years Saller."

15 B. R., XI, 49 (Nov. 9, 1705). See also B. R., XV, 150 (Dec. 21, 1738): "Treasurer Wadsworth has represented to us, that thro' the Deficiency of the Collectors, the Treasury is in great want of money to answer the Draughts that are from time to time made on it—Where by the School masters, Watchmen and other Officers are put to great straits."

16 B. R., XVIII, 258 (Nov. 27, 1776). See also B. R., XVI, 274 (Mar. 13, 1769): "Voted, that the Town Treasurer be and hereby is impowered to give his Negotiable Notes on Interest to the Administrators or Executors of the deceased School Masters, for the Balances respectively due to the said deceased Masters."

greatest part of the Taxes belonging to the Town is already paid in, or engaged to others, so that they have no prospect of any further payment till the new Taxes are issued, which tis probable will not be done till some time in the next Winter—that this delay of payment obliges them to purchase the necessarys of life at a disadvantage Upon long Credit, or to become troublesome to their friends by borrowing Money for their Supplys, not to mention the continual sollicitude and anxiety which such dependant circumstances necessarily create.— The same being read, and duly considered, it appear'd to the Town that the most likely method to answer the end proposed by the Petitioners must be the raising or borrowing a sum of Money sufficient to defray the common and extraordinary charges of the Year; it was therefore

Voted that the sum of Eight Thousand Pounds be raised by a Tax upon the Polls and Estates within this Town for relief of the Poor, and defreying other necessary Charges, arising within the Town the ensuing Year—

.   .   .   .

Voted, that Mr. David Jeffries Treasurer of the Town be an hereby is directed and fully Impower'd to borrow upon Interest of any Person or Persons, a Sum not exceeding Fifteen hundred Pounds lawful Mony, for the Payment of the School-Masters Salarys now due; the wages of the Watch, as also what may be owing to the Master of the Alms House; the Money so borrowed to be repaid in twelve Months out of the £8000—now Voted to be raised by a Tax.[17]

In every year but one, from May 11, 1762, to May 14, 1773, the town treasurer was "directed and Impowered to allow the several Schoolmasters Interest on the Sums due to them from the date of their Warrants to the time of payment."[18]

In times of high prices, some of the salaries were increased in response to petitions from the masters.[19] Payments were made in old tenor during the years 1742–1749, a period of currency depreciation. The situation and the practice are illustrated in the town meeting minutes of May 12, 1747:

The Petition of Mr. Zachariah Hicks master of the North Writing School setting forth that four Years ago he had Two hundred & Eighty Pounds old tenor Bills granted him by the Town for his Support which at that time was to his full content and Satisfaction, but within that course of Years the currency of the province has sunk in its Value to that Degree that the aforesaid Sum is become very far Short of Answering the purpose for which it was designed, and he is thereby Exposed to such Difficulties as are too great an Incumbrance to

[17] B. R., XVI, 73.
[18] B. R., XVI, 95, 116, 146, 186, 214, 247, 284; XVIII, 58, 82, 141.
[19] B. R., VIII, 196 (Mar. 15, 1725/26): Peleg Wiswall was voted an addition of £30, "in Consideration of the Extreme prise of Provisions."

him in the faithful Discharge of his Trust, Praying the Town to Grant him such further allowance as they shall think proper, was now read & after some Debate thereon.—

Voted that the Sum of one hundred Pounds old tenor Bills be Added to M^r. Hicks's Sallary for the Year ensuing, the same to be paid him Quarterly, and to Commence the 22^d. of March last.[20]

At this meeting, "The Petition of Mr John Proctor jun^r. Usher of the North Writing School praying for an Addition to his Salary was taken into Consideration and after some Debate thereon," it was "Voted that the Town will not at present make any Addition to M^r. Proctors Salary."

Until 1758, the grammar school masters usually received the larger stipends.[21] An interesting exception was made in the case of John Proctor, whose salary, as master of the North Writing School, was larger, during the years 1734–1741, than that given to John Lovell, master of the South Grammar School. In 1735, Proctor received an increase of £50, "In consideration of" his "extraordinary Ability, Care, and Diligence in bringing forward the Youth under his Tuition, in the Arts of Writing, Arithmetick &c. the excellent economy of his School, And the Government thereof, As well as the Great Number of his Scholars."[22] According to a record of May 8, 1741, he had "for some time paid an Assistant One Hundred pounds, p. Annum, out of his Salary."[23] Large enrollment was a factor which occasionally influenced the town in its determination of salary allowances to masters whose teaching was satisfactory.[24] Presumably, the same stipends were granted, in 1735, to John Lovell, and to Samuel Holyoke, master of the Writing School in Queen Street. From 1758 to 1771, with the exception of 1762, the master of the South Grammar School received the largest of the school salaries. The reasons for most of the differences, from the earliest years, can only be surmised: the records do not explain all the salary awards.

Occasionally, the master shared his salary with his usher, i.e. the usher was paid by the master, and not directly from the town treasury. "In as much as the Gramer School at the North End of the Town of which m^r Peleg Wiswall is the Master is much increased in the Num-

---

[20] B. R., XIV, 115–16. See also B. R., XIV, 65 (Mar. 25, 1745): Petition of Abiah Holbrook, "Setting forth that his Salary which is now but Two hundred pounds a year old tenor, is not sufficient for his Support and maintenance."

[21] See Appendix A, p. 79, for list of salaries.

[22] B. R., XII, 109 (May 7, 1735).   [23] B. R., XII, 279 (May 8, 1741).

[24] The North Writing School was the largest school in Boston at the time.

ber of the Schollers, and that no Usher is alowed to assist him in his School . . . Voted That there be an Addition of Forty Pounds to the said m^r Wiswalls Salary."[25]

By another arrangement, the master was allowed a certain sum, not called an "Addition to his Salary," which was to be paid to his usher. The town voted, May 15, 1754, "that the Sum of Thirty four Pounds lawful money be Allowed to M^r. Abiah Holbrook Master of the South Writing School in the Common for such Usher as he shall Employ in said School."[26] The amount which the master paid to his usher was determined by the town, or by the selectmen acting on instructions from the town. "It was voted," June 12, 1758, "that the Selectmen be and they hereby are desired to appoint an Assistant to the Master of" the North Grammar School, "and that the Sum of One Hundred and twenty Pounds be allowed for the Yearly Salary of said Master and Assistant, and that such a part thereof be paid to the Assistant as the Selectmen shall agree with him for."[27] In the usual practice, the ushers received their salaries from the town treasury.[28]

When John Tileston, apprentice to Zachariah Hicks, was appointed usher to his master, August 15, 1753, the town voted that Hicks "be paid for his Service as shall be agreed on or allowed by the Selectmen."[29] Tileston's "time," or "hire," belonged to Hicks, and when he received a town appointment, the town was obliged to pay the master for his services. Upon the expiration of his apprenticeship, Tileston received a salary of £50 from the town.[30] In 1761, John Proctor, Junior, master of the Writing School in Queen Street, was "allowed for the hire of his Apprentice James Carter as an Assistant to M^r. Tileston Master of the North Writing School, at the Rate of £34 p. Annum."[31] Carter was voted a stipend of £50, after he had completed his apprenticeship.[32]

---

[25] B. R., XII, 7 (May 6, 1729). See note 23, also B. R., XV, 288 (Apr. 15, 1741), and B. R., XIV, 77 (Mar. 10, 1745/46): Abiah Holbrook asks "that he may be Reimburs'd what he has already paid for Assistance in his School."

[26] B. R., XIV, 260. See also B. R., XVI, 59, 75, 94, 116, 146, 186, 213, 247, 283–84; XVIII, 23–24, 181.

[27] B. R., XVI, 15. See also B. R., XXIII, 213 (Mar. 16, 1774): Andrew Cunningham, appointed usher to Samuel Holbrook, was to "be allowed by him the town's allowance of £34."

[28] B. R., VIII, 63 (Dec. 19, 1709): "Voted. That the Town will defray the Charge of an Assistant" to Nathaniel Williams. See also B. R., VIII, 65 (Mar. 13, 1709/10).

[29] B. R., XIX, 13. Hicks was "allowed" £34.

[30] B. R., XIV, 298 (Mar. 15, 1757).

[31] B. R., XIX, 170 (Dec. 2, 1761).   [32] B. R., XVI, 185 (May 26, 1766).

Salaries were supplemented by "grants," "allowances," and "perquisites." The records indicate that many of the grants were not considered as permanent increases in salaries. Most were awarded for the purpose of relieving temporary financial embarrassments. A few were rewards of merit, as in the case of John Vinal, who was allowed £30 "for his extraordinary services in times past."[33] James Carter, usher in the Writing School in Queen Street, whose salary was £50, received a grant of £25, each year from 1768 to 1773, "as an encouragement for him to exert himself in the Service of the Town."[34] From 1765 to 1774, a similar allowance of £40 was made to James Lovell, whose salary was £60, as usher in the South Grammar School.[35]

Gratuities were also awarded when the town discharged masters or ushers for reasons which did not reflect on ability or character. When the selectmen informed the town, May 3, 1745, "that they Apprehend the Number of Scholars in the North Grammar School so small as that there is no occasion for an Usher," it was voted that the usher "be Continued . . . until the next Quarter is compleat and be paid as heretofore, & then be discharged, and that there be Allowed him the Sum of Thirty pounds old tenor over and above his Salary, as a Gratuity."[36] In view of the circumstances attaching to Daniel Henchman's resignation as usher in the "first Free schoole," he was "allowed £10 ouer and aboue his yeares sallery . . . as a gratuity from the towne for not haueinge suffitient warninge to prouide otherwise for him selfe."[37] Benjamin Tompson, who refused to serve as an usher to Ezekiel Cheever, was given £10 "out of the town treasury beside his yearlie salary."[38]

Illnesses and the infirmities of old age were sympathetically considered by the town. Generous allowances were made, and salaries were voted as usual. A grant of £15 was made to "John Vinal Usher to the South Writing School . . . in consideration of the Straits and Difficultys he has been reduced to by means of Small Pox."[39] In the case of Ephraim Langdon, "the late Usher of the North Grammar School," who had "before he deceased been detained from attending his duty the space of three Months by reason of Bodyly indisposition," the town voted that a

---

[33] B. R., XVI, 76 (May 11, 1762).
[34] B. R., XVI, 247, 283; XVII, 24, 58, 82, 140.
[35] B. R., XVI, 146, 185, 213, 247, 283; XVIII, 23, 58, 81, 140, 180.
[36] B. R., XIV, 73.
[37] B. R., VII, 63 (Nov. 27, 1671).
[38] B. R., VII, 58 (Jan. 30, 1670/71).
[39] B. R., XVI, 118–19 (May 15, 1764).

"Draft shall be made on the Treasury for the amount of the Deceased Salary the Time he was absent from School, payable to the Administrator."[40]

One of the selectmen was appointed, December 16, 1766, "to wait upon Master Wissell & desire him not to expose his health by attending School this Winter . . . his Salary shall be drawn for notwithstanding."[41] Peleg Wiswall was then eighty-three years of age, and had "great Infermities." In the following February, the selectmen persuaded him to resign: "He said he was sensible of the difficulties coming on before his last confinement & that he had for some Weeks past thought it his duty to let the Selectmen know his infirmities would prevent his further attendance upon the business of said School and after some further discourse resigned the place as Master of said School; adding that he had spent his Estate in the Towns service and hoped they would not let him suffer to which it was reply'd by them that the disposition of the Town was such that we could not doubt he would be provided for during the remainder of his Days."[42] The town then "Voted, that the Sum of One hundred Pounds be and hereby is granted to M^r. Peleg Wiswell, for his support the ensuing year."[43]

Dwellings, owned by the town, were provided for some of the masters. The selectmen's minutes, of March 29, 1652, refer to the "Libertie" granted to Richard Cook, "to set a house one the Towne's ground, which is betwixt the towne's house in which M^r. Woodmansy now liveth, and the town schoole house."[44] The "towne's house" may have been occupied by Woodbridge in 1645.[45] Woodmansey lived in this house at the time of his death, August 13, 1667.[46] Two years later, his widow was informed by one of the selectmen "that the towne occasions

[40] B. R., XX, 192 (July 1, 1766).

[41] B. R., XX, 240.

[42] B. R., XX, 243 (Feb. 5, 1767).

[43] B. R., XVI, 200 (Mar. 9, 1767). He died Sept. 2, 1767. Wiswall was the only schoolmaster of Boston who was granted a retiring allowance during the colonial period. John Tileston was pensioned in 1819.

[44] B. R., II, 109. See also B. R., II, 116 (June 27, 1653): 40 shillings to Woodmansey, "as part of his repayres to his house."

[45] B. R., II, 86 (Oct. 28, 1645). See p. 96, *infra*. It should be noted that the "garden plott" assigned to Daniel Maude, Apr. 17, 1637, was merely one of the town allotments to the inhabitants of Boston (B. R., II, 17), and not an allowance for the support of a schoolmaster.

[46] B. R., II, 142 (Jan. 25, 1657): "the house belonging to the schoole shall bee repaired;" 148 (July 26, 1658): "Woodmansyes house shall bee sufficiently repayred before winter."

need the vse of the schoole house," and that she should "prouide otherwise for her selfe."[47] Mrs. Woodmansey requested that she be supplied with "a house to live in, if she remoueth from the schoole house," to which the town responded that it would "allowe her £8. p. an for that end, dureing her widdowhood."[48]

The records suggest that Ezekiel Cheever lived in the "schoole [dwelling] house," and not in rooms in the building which was used for instruction.[49] On January 6, 1670/71, Benjamin Tompson "declared his remouall to Charlestowne," and "resigned vp the possession of the schoole & schoole house . . . And it was further agreed that the said Mr Cheeuers should be allowed sixtie pounds p. an for his seruice in the school out of the towne rates & rents that be longe to the schoole, and the possession & vse of ye schoole house."[50] After many years of occupancy by the masters of the school, the house was in such a state of disrepair that the town was moved, March 11, 1699/1700, to "Consider about repairing or Building, or hiring a House for Mr Ezek^ll Cheever."[51] A year later, it was "Voted That a House be Built for Old m^r. Ezek. Cheever;" and two of the selectmen were "appointed to provide a House for Mr Chever to dwell in untill a house be built for him."[52] From May 3, 1701, until October or November, 1702, when the new building was completed, Cheever lived in a house rented for him by the town.[53] Upon his appointment as master, Nathaniel Williams was "invited to remove into ye House where Mr Cheever dwelt."[54] After 1734, the house was occupied by John Lovell, who succeeded Williams.[55]

During the incumbency of Edward Mills, the town appropriated a dwelling for the master of the Writing School in Queen Street. The first master, John Cole, lived in a rented house, for which the town

[47] B. R., VII, 51 (Dec. 27, 1669).

[48] B. R., VII, 53 (Mar. 14, 1669/70). In these two records, "the schoole house" was "the towne's house," mentioned in 1652, a dwelling separate from the school building.

[49] Jenks and later writers say that he lived in the school building.

[50] B. R., VII, 57.

[51] B. R., VII, 241; VIII, 4. See also B. R., XI, 8 (Aug. 25, 1701): "Mr Ezekiell Chever is allowed fifty Six Shillings for Severall years repaires of his house School house as p his acco^t."

[52] B. R., VII, 244 (Mar. 10, 1700/1); XI, 3 (Apr. 28, 1701).

[53] B. R., XI, 8 (Aug. 25, 1701), 11 (Nov. 24, 1701), 17 (Mar. 2, 1701/2), 20 (Mar. 30, 1702), 22 (May 12, 1702), 27 (Sept. 28, 1702). See Appendix B, p. 89, for location and description of the house.

[54] B. R., XI, 79 (Sept. 6, 1708). See also B. R., VIII, 76; XIII, 66, 69, 100; XII, 26.

[55] B. R., XV, 137 (Sept. 20, 1738): "the Towns House where m^r. John Lovell dwells in School Street;" XVI, 88, 93; XX, 220.

made him an allowance.[56] Cole's successor, Jacob Sheafe, preferred to live at "his father's house . . . near" the South Writing School.[57] After the death of Edward Mills, Samuel Holyoke was permitted "to haue the use of the House Mr Mills lived in."[58] In turn, this house was occupied by John Proctor, Junior, and James Carter.[59] Proctor's colleague, Samuel Holbrook, did not live in a dwelling provided by the town, nor did he receive an allowance for rent.

Some of the masters lived in houses which they rented. They received compensation, however, in the form of rent-allowances voted by the town. The records mention grants of £4 lawful money to £70 old tenor, "for ye Hire of a House," to Richard Henchman, master of the North Writing School, and to John Barnard, Peleg Wiswall, and Samuel Hunt, masters of the North Grammar School.[60] Only one of the ushers was considered in connection with his rent. In response to the "Petition of Mr. Zech. Hicks," the town voted, March 11, 1734/35, "That the sum of Twenty Pounds be allow'd & paid to the said Mr. Hicks in Consideration of his House Rent, and in Addition to his Salary for this year."[61] There appears to have been no provision of dwellings or rent, during the colonial period, for the masters of the South Writing School.[62]

In addition to the various grants, certain perquisites were allowed the masters. The earliest reference to these occurs in a letter from Samuel Sewall to Increase Mather, April 25, 1710: "At the last Anniversary Meeting the Town augmented the Masters Salary to One Hundred pounds p. annum. What with that, and some small perquisits, a humble

[56] B. R., VIII, 104–5 (May 17, 1714): Upon his resignation, the town voted him a "grant" of "Two pounds and Sixteen Shillings in Consideration of what he formerly pd for the Rent of his School-House."

[57] B. R., XIII, 100 (July 11, 1722).

[58] B. R., XII, 41 (Mar. 13, 1732/33). See also B. R., XIII, 240.

[59] B. R., XX, 296 (June 15, 1768): "the widow of said Master Holyoke having removed;" XXIII, 214 (Mar. 23, 1774): "the House the widow of the late M^r. Procter lived in is now empty." Evidently, the widows were not forced to vacate their homes immediately. A record of Mar. 12, 1779 (B. R., XXVI, 58) refers to Carter's "House being found by the Town."

[60] B. R., XI, 4 (Apr. 28, 1701), 10 (Nov. 24, 1701), 17 (Mar. 6, 1701/2), 22 (May 25, 1702), 36 (Nov. 29, 1703); VIII, 104 (May 14, 1714), 110 (Mar. 14, 1714/15), 119 (Mar. 13, 1715/16), 126 (May 15, 1717), 143 (Mar. 15, 1719/20); XIV, 135 (Mar. 15, 1747/48); XVIII, 158 (Mar. 5, 1774).

[61] B. R., XII, 101. This action was not repeated.

[62] B. R., XXVI, 57 (Mar. 12, 1779): Samuel Holbrook granted £30 "in consideration of his House Rent."

Christian Man that loves Work more than Wages, needs not be discouraged."[63] When John Lovell was appointed master of the South Grammar School, May 21, 1734, the town "Voted, That the Stipend, Pay or Salary, with the Emoluments of the said School now belonging to the Rev. Mr. Williams, the present Master thereof, Shall be and belong to the said Mr. Lovel."[64] The nature of these "Emoluments" is revealed in John Proctor's reply to "the Complaint of his refusing to take the Children of some Families of low Circumstances in the World, and insisting on large demands for Firing & Entry money &c.," in which "he Informed that as to Firing, he had not more than Five Shillings a piece, one with another (some paying and some not) and as to the Entry money, he has not Demanded any of the Town Inhabitants, but of Strangers, of which he has now about Ten in his School, And that . . . if he had not the whole of the Perquisites, he could not keep the School."[65] The selectmen reported to the town, May 8, 1741, that there were "about Two Hundred and Eighty Scholars" at John Proctor's school.[66] At "Five Shillings a piece," the fire-money amounted to £70. This sum, in the depreciated currency of the time, would not have purchased a year's supply of wood for Proctor's dwelling and schoolhouse. In 1751, the selectmen were ordered to set the fee which the masters might demand for "firing."[67] Neither this nor the amount of the entrance fee appears in the town records.

Samuel Holbrook, upon his appointment as one of the masters of the Writing School in Queen Street, August 1, 1753, was "allowed Sixty Pounds p. annum, and also allowed to improve the School for his own advantage out of School hours, and to be entitled to the Perquisites of the School (the Fire money excepted)."[68] His successor, John Proctor, Junior, received a salary of £70, and "one half the Perquisites of the School (the Fire Money excepted) . . . also . . . the improvement of the School out of School-hours."[69] Proctor was obliged to share the perquisites with the other master of the school.

[63] *Coll. Mass. Hist. Soc.*, 6th Series, I, 391–93.

[64] B. R., XII, 86. After the reversion of Thomas Gunter's lease, Lovell was permitted, May 20, 1772, to "have the use of the Cellar under the South Grammar School" (B. R., XVIII, 81). He may have had an income from it.

[65] B. R., XV, 288 (Apr. 15, 1741).

[66] B. R., XII, 279.

[67] B. R., XIV, 199 (May 14, 1751). "Entrance & Fire Money" were abolished by a town vote of Apr. 5, 1784. Firewood was provided by the town (B. R., XXXI, 18).

[68] B. R., XVII, 299. The salary of Samuel Holyoke, the other master, was £80.

[69] B. R., XIX, 12 (Aug. 9, 1754).

By making ink themselves, the masters may have been able to save a small sum from the town's ink allowance, that is, when it was paid.[70] The town voted, March 23, 1753, that Abiah Holbrook, master of the South Writing School, "provide the Scholars under his Care with Ink as he requests in his Petition, provided he will do it for Four Pounds Lawful Money a Year."[71] Thirteen years later, he "applied to the Selectmen to have a Draft for Supply of Ink agreeable to the Vote of the Town for Eight years past, it not having been drawn for since May, 1758."[72] His brother, Samuel Holbrook, master of the Writing School in Queen Street, August 1, 1753—August 1, 1754, was allowed only "Twenty Shillings . . . for Supplying the Scholars with Ink during the Time he was Master."[73]

From the diary of John Tileston, it may be inferred that the masters were permitted to sell paper, pencils, quills, and copy-books to their pupils.[74] A small but steady income was realized from these items.

The most profitable of the perquisites was "the improvement of the School out of School-hours." Masters who desired it were granted the privilege of using the school buildings for the instruction of private pupils, at hours which did not conflict with the regular schedule of the public schools. Abiah Holbrook was given "Liberty . . . to keep a private School to teach youth the Rules of Psalmody Agreeable to his Petition therefor."[75] His "singing School" was open only "during the Summer Season."[76] In the winter, his usher, John Vinal, conducted evening classes in writing and arithmetic "at the South-Writing-School."[77] Some of the masters must have added an appreciable sum to their incomes by giving private instruction.

---

[70] John Tileston's diary, entry of Apr. 9, 1764: "Ingredients for 1 quart of Ink—4 ounces of Galls of Aleppo, 2 ounces of Copperas, 2 ounces of Gum Arabic" (Colesworthy, D. C., *John Tileston's School; also his diary from 1761 to 1766*. Boston, 1887, p. 72).

[71] B. R., XIV, 234. See also B. R., XIV, 230-31 (Mar. 13, 1753).

[72] B. R., XX, 216 (May 26, 1766). See also B. R., XIX, 73 (Jan. 30, 1758): "A draft for Ink for the Schools."

[73] B. R., XIV, 216 (Aug. 7, 1754).

[74] *Op. cit.*, 72: "Sept. 16 [1764] Bought of Capt'n Boroughs . . . ten thousand quills at 45s. per thousand . . . likewise . . . 4 thousand for Master Proctor. . . . Oct. 10 [1764] Made 5½ books, best paper."

[75] B. R., XVII, 76 (Aug. 1, 1744). As already noted, this privilege was given to Samuel Holbrook and John Proctor, Junior.

[76] *Boston Gazette*, June 26, 1744.

[77] *Ibid*, Sept. 13, 27, 1756; B. R., XIX, 145 (Apr. 15, 1761). John Tileston's diary mentions his "evening School," and "private scholars" (*op. cit.*, 72).

An interesting comment on the colonial practice appears in the report of "The Comittee appointed to consider of a future Arangement of the free Schools in this Town," April 5, 1784:

Moreover the Practice of the School-Masters in instructing the same Children who are intitled to the Benefit of the publick Schools, at other Hours than those devoted to the Town hath a Tendency to draw their Attention from the Publick to the private Schools, to incite an odious Distinction between those whose Parents can Afford the Expence of their Attending the private Schools & those who cannot.—And it greatly increases the General Expence of Education.—It is therefore the Opinion of the Committee that the Schoolmasters employed by the Town ought not to teach such of the Male Children of the Inhabitants as are under the Age of fourteen years, in the same branches of Learning at their private and the publick Schools—

If the foregoing Opinions of the Committee respecting the Practice of the Schoolmasters shall meet the Approbation of the Town, they will in that case be abridged of certain Perquisites which they have heretofore received, with, at least the tacit Consent of the Town; and therefore the Committee beg leave to recommend to the Consideration of the Town Whether such Adition should not be made to their Salaries as to enable them to support their own Children & Families and in the Exercise of that Cardinal Virtue, Prudence to lay up for them such a Moderate Overplus, as every industrious & provident Inhabitant wishes to do for his own Family at the Period of Needfulness or Life—But if the Town should think it proper that the practice should continue with Respect to the Instruction of any of the Children at what are called private Hours, the Committee recommend that the terms of Instruction at such Hours be regulated by the Selectmen or a standing Committee for regulating the Schools.[78]

The "Report having been read and considered," the town "Voted, that the Selectmen be directed not to employ or Continue any Person as a Publick Schoolmaster or Usher who shall not agree to have the Terms of Instruction of the Children of the Town at Private hours regulated by the Selectmen."[79] Apparently, the town was not ready to grant large increases in salaries.

In order to encourage grammar school masters, the General Court granted them exemption from poll and estate taxes.[80] This statute, re-enacted almost every year from 1692 to 1775, did not refer to the writing school masters. In this connection, as the following petition indicates, the law seems to have been rather liberally construed by the town, or its agents:

[78] B. R., XXXI, 17.
[79] B. R., XXXI, 18.
[80] *Acts and Resolves of the Prov. of the Mass. Bay*, I, 29 (June 24, 1692), and vols. ff.

The Petition of Edward Mills of Boston

Humbly Sheweth

That Whereas the Governm^t of this Province have been the singular Patrons of liberall Education and use many wayes to encourage all Tutors and Students therein & particularly by an Act for Apportioning & Assessing of Taxes &c: Have (amongst others) extended immunities therefrom to Gramm^r School Masters, who have ever had the benefit of that exemption, & All still have it except yor Petitioner Who, tho he has Sent Sundry Students from his School to Colledge, & been serving the Town in the capacity of a Gramm^r Tutour for the space of near Twenty Years, is made now a Single instance, by Assessing not only his School House but even his Poll &c^a While meer Writeing Masters in this Town are (some from all Taxes, Others from ye Poll) excused.

Yo^r Petitioner therefore Prays Yo^r Hono^rs favourable consideration that he may injoy those incouragem^ts wch he humbly conceives himself intituled to, either by a clause to be added to the Act Relating to School Masters whereby yor Petitioner may be intituled to the full benefit of s^d Act or otherwise as to your grave Wisdomes shall seem meet.

The Court ordered, November 8, 1710, "that he be exempted from public Taxes, in manner as Grammar Schoolmasters are by Law."[81]

If Mills's testimony is reliable, the town assessors used their own discretion in the matter of taxing the writing school masters of his day. The only recorded petition of this sort from one of the public writing school masters was disregarded by the town.[82]

The records contain many petitions for allowances and additions to salaries. As one might expect, some of the masters petitioned periodically. Although there were complaints of inadequacy and delay, the salaries of the schoolmasters were usually higher than those of the various town officials.

---

[81] *Mass. Archives*, LVIII, 278; *Acts and Resolves*, IX, 150 (Nov. 8, 1710). Mills conducted a private school at this time.

[82] B. R., XVI, 207 (Mar. 23, 1767): Abiah Holbrook asks for consideration "with respect to his Taxes."

CHAPTER VII

SUPERVISION

THROUGHOUT the colonial period, the public schools of Boston were administered by the town.[1] Schools were established and sources of income were designated by the vote of the "Freeholders and other Inhabitants." The town, or the selectmen instructed by the town, appointed the masters and ushers, and determined salaries and allowances. For the purpose of expediting the details of school operation, the town delegated authority to the selectmen. As agents of the town, they were responsible for the active supervision of the schools.[2]

During the seventeenth and early eighteenth centuries, supervision was carried on by occasional visitation. Much of the inspection was quite informal, the selectmen visiting singly, or otherwise, whenever they saw fit. As circumstances warranted, the town or the selectmen considered the various needs of the schools, and voted special investigations.

For reasons not revealed in the records, the town voted, December 19, 1709, "That a Committee be chosen to consider of the affaires relateing to the Grāmer Free School of this Town, & to make report thereof."[3] At the town meeting of March 13, 1709/10, the committee submitted the following suggestion:

We further propose and recommend as of Great Service and Advantage for the promoting of Diligence and good literature, That the Town Agreeably to the Usage in England, and (as we understand) in Some time past practiced here, Do Nominate and Appoint a Certain Number of Gentlemen, of Liberal Education, Together with Some of yᵉ Revᵈ Ministers of the Town to be Inspectors of the Sᵈ Schoole under that name Title or denomination, To Visit yᵉ School from time to time, when and as Oft, as they shall thinck fit to Enform themselves of the methodes used in teaching of yᵉ Scholars and to Inquire of their Proficiency, And be present at the performance of Some of their Exercises, the Master being before Notified of their Comeing, And with him to consult

---

[1] Governor Andros usurped some of the authority of the town, in school matters, during his administration. After his removal, the town voted, June 3, 1689, "that the former Custome & practice in managing the affaires of the free schools be restored & continued."

[2] The selectmen were reminded, Mar. 14, 1663/64, that the authority on all matters of public concern was in the town meeting (B. R., VII, 20–21).

[3] B. R., VIII, 63.

and Advise of further Methods for yᵉ Advancement of Learning and the Good Government of the Schoole.[4]

Upon considering "the Said Report in the Several Articles thereof," the town voted "to mak: choice of [five] Inspectors according to the aforesaid proposalls . . . to Serve for one year ensuing." Although the recommendation refers to a "usage . . . in Some time past practiced here," the action of this meeting established the first "Inspectors" of the grammar school.[5]

Before this time, the ministers had played a part in the visitation of the school. The records do not indicate whether they did so on their own initiative or by invitation of the town or selectmen. Cotton Mather decided, on June 7, 1699, to "visit all the schools; and endeavor to speak such things both to the Teachers and the Scholars, as they may all bee the better for!"[6] In May, 1718, he noted that "a fresh visitation of our Schools, will give me now some Opportunities for the Doing of Good more Wayes than one."[7] His special attention was given to the North Grammar School, which was near his home.[8] According to the records, he was invited to attend but one of the annual visitations.[9] Apparently, the other visits were wholly gratuitous.

There were no ministers among the inspectors appointed March 13, 1709/10: Waite Winthrop, Samuel Sewall, Elisha Cooke, Isaac Addington, and Thomas Brattle. This action so displeased Increase Mather, pastor of the Second Church, that he expressed his disapproval in a letter to Samuel Sewall, April 24, 1710:

Sir, I understand that there is a discourse about Visitors for the School, and that your self intends to speak with me about that Affair, and to desire that I would be concerned. I therefore send this to prevent you from that trouble; for I am not willing to be concerned; for 2 Reasons; 1. I have no Call to that Service. I cannot but judge that the Ministers of the Town are the fittest persons in the World to be the Visitors of the School. But the Town (I hear) has left them out of their Vote; which has been a great disrespect, and Contempt put upon (not me but) all the Ministers in Boston. They must be very fond of the Office (which I am sure I am not) who shall now run before they are called. A

---

[4] B. R., VIII, 65. This action did not reflect upon the ability of Nathaniel Williams, "the present master of whos: qualifications and fitness for that imployment we tak: for granted everybody must be abundantly Satisfied" (B. R., VIII, 64–65).

[5] The records contain no reference to an earlier usage of this sort.

[6] The Diary of Cotton Mather, in *Coll. Mass. Hist. Soc.*, 7th Series, VII, 304.

[7] *Ibid*, VIII, 533.

[8] *Ibid*, VIII, 236, 472, 531, 548–49, 580.

[9] B. R., XIII, 153 (June 17, 1726): invited for June 24, 1726.

Secondary call from T. B. &c. I esteem as none at all. 2. I am stricken in years. That which was a Recreation to me formerly, is now a Burden. I may not then concern myself with a new office . . .

Nevertheless, I purpose (if God will) to goe to the Schoolhouse, and preach a Sermon to the children; but not as a Visitor. And therefore I am not willing that any one should goe with me (especially not any of the Visitors chosen by the Town) For which cause I shall conceal the day of my doing that Service from every-body, untill the work is over.[10]

Judge Sewall replied immediately, as follows:

Rever.d Sir, I am favoured with yours of yesterday. The purpose there mentioned, I Entreat you to Review, and alter . . . As for the business of the Visitation, the Town also came into that, with this caution, that the Visitors should stand but one year. And I am confident, they designed not to offend, much less to contemn any of the honoured Pastors. But many times you know, *In vitium ancit culpae fuga.* For which, in their behalf, I ask your Pardon. Four of this year's Visitors were bred and born in the Town, and bear a considerable part of its charge. Mr. Brattle is a good Scholar, and excells in Mathematical Learning, upon which Account Respect is due to him. As for any Exorbitances of his, the Town is far from abetting him in them. And therefore I humbly entreat you to do what Service you shall chuse, for the School; only condescend to do it upon the Tenth of May, the Time apointed by the Visitors: your work will thereby be much more Beautifull, much more Honourable, much more profitable. Boston of the Massachusets invites you, calls you, Courts you.[11]

As Sewall stated, the visitors were to "stand" for one year only, but, at the meetings of March 12, 1710/11 and March 10, 1712/13, the same men were "chosen to be Inspectors of the Free Gramer School for the year ensueing."[12] At the latter meeting, the town "Voted. That a Committee Shall be raised to Inspect the Free writing Schools which are Supported at the Townes Charge, And . . . That John Clark Esq.r, Coll.o Adam Winthrop & Major Thomas Fitch be the S.d Comittee."[13] Again, the town expressed its dissent from Mather's opinion that the ministers were "the fittest persons in the World to be the Visitors."

In the following year, the ministers were included: the town voted "That y.e Sel: men together with the Reverend Ministers of this Town be desired to be the Inspectors of the Free Grammar Schools for the year ensuing."[14] This vote, with similar phraseology, was repeated at

---

[10] The Letter-Book of Samuel Sewall, in *Coll. Mass. Hist. Soc.*, 6th Series, I, 393–94.

[11] *Ibid*, I, 391–93.

[12] B. R., VIII, 75, 95. Inspectors were not elected at the meeting of Mar. 10, 1711/12. Probably the earlier group continued to serve.

[13] B. R., VIII, 94 (Mar. 9, 1712/13).   [14] B. R., VIII, 100 (Mar. 16, 1713/14).

the next four annual meetings.[15] The ministers were chosen again, at the meeting of March 9, 1718/19, but they were to serve with a committee of seven men, only one of whom was a selectman.[16] These seven were re-elected March 15, 1719/20; the ministers were not mentioned.[17] The omission of the writing schools after March 9, 1712/13 is not significant: no doubt they were included in the annual visitations. From March 13, 1720/21 until the end of the colonial period, the town voted annually "that the Select men and Such as they Shall desire to Assist them be Inspectors . . . of the Schools for the year ensuing."[18] Throughout this time, the selectmen regularly invited the ministers and others to accompany them.

As the years went on, the visitation committee grew until it numbered fifty or sixty who actually attended on the day of the annual visit. At times, it included the Governor, Lieutenant Governor, members of the Council, Representatives to the General Court, the overseers of the poor, the selectmen, the ministers, judges, and many others.[19] An account of Jonathan Belcher's visit of June 19, 1734, may be of interest:

Last Wednesday being the Day appointed by the Select Men for the Visitation of the Free Schools in this Town, they resolved to attend that Service with some of the Ministers of the Town as usual. His Excellency Governor Belcher being apprised of their Resolution, took that opportunity of paying the Schools a Visit, at the same time to shew his Respect to the Town, and give his Countenance and Encouragement to Learning among us. At the two Grammar Schools his Excellency was Saluted by the two Masters in Latin Orations, to which his Excellency returned his Answer in Latin, as elegantly as kindly. His Excellency being gratified with the Reception which he had met with at these and the other Schools and pleas'd with the Improvement of the Children in them, directed the Masters respectively to allow their Scholars a Play Day; and then Invited the Masters, together with the Visitors of the Schools, to an Entertainment in the Evening.[20]

If Governor Belcher was invited, it must have been an afterthought. His name does not appear in the list of those who were "desired," at a meeting of June 5, 1734, "to Accompany the Select Men on that Serv-

---

[15] B. R., VIII, 109 (Mar. 21, 1714/15), 117 (Mar. 12, 1715/16), 124 (Mar. 11, 1716/17), 129 (Mar. 10, 1717/18).

[16] B. R., VIII, 136.

[17] B. R., VIII, 142.

[18] B. R., VIII, 151. The phrasing varies but slightly from year to year.

[19] See Appendix C, p. 91. Occasional attendance by successful private school masters and former public school masters insured capable inspection.

[20] *Boston Gazette*, June 17–24, 1734; *Boston Weekly News-Letter*, June 20–27, 1734.

ice, and to meet at the Town House, at 9 of the Clock in the morning."[21] The selectmen may have permitted the Governor to act as host
at "an Entertainment in the Evening." They had already voted, however, "That a Dinner be provided at Mrs. Wardalls, and the afore mentioned Gentlemen, with the several School Masters be Invited to Dine
with us."[22]

As early as June 5, 1733, the selectmen voted that a "Dinner be provided" for the school visitors.[23] Although the records of 1733–1774
refer to but eighteen visitation dinners, they may have been provided
annually. The masters were specifically invited to attend the dinners of
1733, 1734, and 1739.[24] At a selectmen's meeting, June 11, 1765,
"M^r. Williston was directed to call upon M^r. Wiswall & M^r. Lovel,
the Masters of the two public Grammar Schools for the Names of the
Fathers of those Children who are In their highest Forms, and will
leave School this Season, that those Parents may be invited to attend the
Visitation, and dine at Faneuil Hall on said Day."[25]

By 1764, these entertainments had outgrown the accommodations at
Mrs. Wardwell's, or the Orange Tree Tavern, where they were usually
held. In that year, the selectmen voted "That a Dinner be provided at
Faneuil Hall for about 50 Gentlemen on the Day for visiting the Schools,
and that M^r. Ballard shall have the dressing thereof, and also furnish
the Liquors that may be wanted."[26] On "account of the present distress," in 1774, "the dinner usual on such days was laid aside."[27]

The nature of the inspection is indicated in the visitation report submitted to the town, March 19, 1738/39:

The Report of the Select Men of the Visitation of the Public Schools, being Presented, was Read, as follows. Viz^t.

To the Inhabitants of Boston, Town Meeting assembled,
Mar. 12, 1738
Pursuant to a Vote of the Town of Boston at their annual meeting the 13th.

[21] B. R., XIII, 254. This visitation, appointed for Tuesday, June 18, may have been
postponed to June 19, when the selectmen learned that the Governor would be
pleased to attend on that date.

[22] Voted June 5.

[23] B. R., XIII, 241.

[24] The ushers were included, in 1739.

[25] B. R., XX, 161. This is the only invitation to the parents which appears in the
town records.

[26] B. R., XX, 84 (July 6, 1764).

[27] B. R., XXIII, 222 (July 6, 1774). The "present distress" was an epidemic of small-
pox.

of March, 1737. Desiring Us the Select Men to Visit the several Public Schools in the Town, &c.—

We accordingly Attended that Service on the 26th. of June last past, Accompanied by the following Gentlemen, Viz^t.

> The Hon. Thomas Hutchinson Esqr.
> The Hon. Adam Winthrop Esqr.
> The Hon. Ezekiel Lewis Esqr.
> The Hon. Anthony Stoddard Esqr.
> The Hon. Jacob Wendell Esqr.
> The Rev. Mr. William Hooper
> The Rev. Mr. Samuel Mather.

And now Report, as follows.

That the Number of Scholars instructed in the Public Schools is as follows, Viz^t.

In the South Grammar School, about One Hundred and Twenty.
In the North Grammar School, about Sixty.
In the North Writing School, about Two Hundred & Eighty.
In the Writing School in Queen Street, about Seventy three.
In the South Writing School, about Sixty two.—

That We heard the Performances of the Lattin Scholars at each Grammar School, And inspected the Performances of the Scholars in the other Schools, both in Writing and Arithmetick, And heard the younger Scholars read—And that in general they perform'd to the great satisfaction of the Visitors—And We have grounds to hope that the Masters in the said several Schools do faithfully Dischardge the Trust reposed in them.

And We look upon it as a point of Justice due to the Master of the South Writing School, to Report, that the Writing both of the Master and Scholars has been of late much improved.—

> John Jeffries.
> Jon^a. Armitage.
> David Collson.
> Alex^a. Forsyth.   Select Men.
> Caleb Lyman.
> Jonas Clarke.
> Thos. Hutchinson Junr.

Voted, That the Report of the Select Men, of the Visitation of the Schools, now Read, be Accepted—

Voted, That the Select Men be, and hereby are Desired to Visit the Public Schools within the Town, the year ensuing, Desiring such Gentlemen to accompany them therein, as they shall think proper, And that they Report thereon.[28]

[28] B. R., XII, 212–13. Meeting assembled March 12, adjourned to March 19.

Reports of the annual visitations, which were usually made late in June or early in July, were presented at the town meetings in the following spring.[29]

The annual visitation reports from March 19, 1738/39 to May 10, 1774, constitute our chief source of information concerning "the Number of Scholars instructed in the Public Schools." For the years 1635–1739, there is but one record which indicates the number of students enrolled in any of the public schools. On March 13, 1709/10, "The Committee chosen by the Town the 19th of December Last, to consider the Affaires relating to ye Free Grammer School of this Town" expressed the opinion that "the worke of that School do's necessarily require the Attendance of a master and an Usher, and it seems Impracticable for one person alone, well to Oversee the manners of So great a number of Scholars (oft times more than a hundred)."[30] If the selectmen made regular "returns" in the earlier period, the statistics were not entered in the minutes of the town or of the selectmen. A complete report does not appear in the records until March 19, 1738/39.[31] The statistics appear on the following page.[32]

Verifiable population statistics will not permit a satisfactory estimate of the proportion of the total population enrolled in the schools. The total white population of Boston in 1742 was 15,008.[33] In that year, there were 535—3.56 per cent—attending the schools. The school enrollment in 1765 was 6.26 per cent of the white population.[34]

In addition to the annual visitations, the town found it necessary, at times, to order a "particular Enquiry": the selectmen were "desired to Visit the several Schools in the Town, and particularly Enquire into their State & Circumstances, and the proficiency of the Scholars that attend at said Schools, and report thereon as soon as may be."[35] The

[29] The thirty-four reports which contain enrollment statistics attach to visitations made on the following dates: June 17 (1), 19 (2), 22 (3), 23 (2), 24 (1), 25 (5), 26 (2), 27 (1), 28 (3), 29 (3); July 1 (3), 4 (2), 5 (2), 6 (1), 7 (1), 11 (2). Until 1745, the reports were presented at the March meeting; after that date, at the May meeting.

[30] B. R., VIII, 65.

[31] Reproduced on p. 62, *supra*.

[32] The arrangement is mine. Initials are used to indicate the South Grammar School, North Grammar School, South Writing School, North Writing School, and the Writing School in Queen Street. See Appendix D, p. 93, for sources, which are attached to the appropriate dates.

[33] B. R., XV, 369 (Dec. 14, 1742). Total: 16,382. Negroes: 1374.

[34] B. R., XX, 170 (July 29, 1765). Total: 15,520. Negroes and Indians: 848. "White People under Sixteen": males, 4109; females, 4010.

[35] B. R., XIV, 65–66 (Mar. 25, 1744/45).

	S. G. S.	N. G. S.	S. W. S.	N. W. S.	W. S. Q. St.	Totals
1738	"about" 120	"about" 60	"about" 62	"about" 280	"about" 73	c. 595
1739	110	66	60	280	77	593
1740	85	60	53	270	83	551
1741	87	65	48	200	74	474
1742	94	65	73	230	73	535
1743	"about" 90	65	160	"upwards of" 200	"about" 70	c. 585
1744	107		140	200		474+
1745	124	40	171	259	68	662
1746	109	35	240	250	61	695
1747	110	40	265	271	62	748
1748	120	38	270	270	57	755
1749	120	45	278	250	72	765
1750	117	43	260	267	93	780
1751	120	49	270	265	90	794
1753	120	43	320	280	85	848
1754	120	40	220	240	180	800
1755	125	28	216	210	180	759
1756	128	32	224	225	180	789
1757	115	36	240	220	230	841
1758	107	35	230	224	230	826
1759	117	33	220	220	225	815
1761	117	57	234	157	249	814
1762	119	68	236	176	238	837
1763	135	53	230	174	238	830
1764	120	47	230	163	148	708
1765	119	47	250	246	246	908
1766	145	34	260	256	222	917
1767	147	35	270	284	217	953
1768	141	55	201	260		657+
1769	142	60	203	253	251	909
1770	137	56	231	250	268	942
1771	138	61	210	264	268	941
1772	130	59	220	250	264	923
1773	139	60		240	280	719+

selectmen were instructed not only to "Enquire into the behaviour of the Scholars and the Government and Regulation they are under, and give such Directions to the Masters of said Schools concerning them, as they shall judge needful," but also to ascertain "whether there is any Neglect of Duty in the Masters or Ushers of said Schools."[36]

Following such a "particular Enquiry," Ames Angier was dismissed from his position as master of the South Writing School, May 15, 1722:

The Return of the Com̃ittee about m^r Ames Anger & the South School vizt.

Pursuant to the directions of the freeholders & Inhabitants of the Town at their Annual meeting in March last.

[36] B. R., XIV, 233 (Mar. 23, 1753); XVI, 11 (May 16, 1758); XII, 306 (Sept. 13, 1742): One of the selectmen moved "that the Town would take into their Consideration some proper Method for the better Government & Regulation of the North Writing School."

Co^ll Pen Townsend, Jeramiah Allen Esqr, & John Edwards together with the Select men. Vissitted the wrighting School at the Southerly End of Boston on Thirsday the 24th ap^ll 1722. and Examined the Scholars under m^r Ames Angers tuition as to their proficiency in Reading writing Scyphering & the masters ability of teaching & Instructing youth & his Rules & methods therefore. And are of Opinion That it will be no Service to the Town to Continue m^r Anger in that Employ.[37]

Before considering Jeremiah Condy's request for an "Addition to his Salary," the town "desired" that its committee "in an Espesial Mañer Vizit m^r Condys School and Report to the Town at their Meeting the Ability and Industry of the said m^r Condy and the Proficiency of the Scholars under his Tuition."[38] On another occasion, a visitation committee was instructed to "direct m^r Peter Blin to a more Constant & diligent application to the dischardge of the Trust Comitted to him."[39]

Desiring something more convincing than the usual report submitted by the selectmen, the town voted, March 29, 1734, "That the several Writing Masters . . . do present, at the next General Town Meeting, Some of their own performances in Writing, for the Town's inspection."[40] A criticism of the effectiveness of the supervision carried on by the selectmen appears in a proposal submitted to the town meeting of May 7, 1735:

That there be a Committee specially Appointed to make strict Enquiry into the Ability and Learning of the Masters of the Free Writing Schools within this Town, and what Proficiency the Children under their Care have made, or are like to attain in Reading, Writing and Arithmetick For as the want of Able and Accurate Masters in Initiating Youth in the Rudiments of Learning will prove fatal and prevent the true design of Education—It is therefore hoped that as this Town has appeared Generous in the Encouraging Learning and good Literature, it will ever be Supply'd with School Masters Equal to such an Excellent Employment, And that they may be duly and honourably Encouraged.[41]

To this, the selectmen replied "That the Town has always been in the

---

37 B. R., VIII, 164.

38 B. R., XII, 8 (May 6, 1729). There were no ministers on this committee.

39 B. R., XII, 14 (Mar. 9, 1729/30). Among the "directions," voted by the selectmen, May 25, 1719, for "the Masters of the Free writeing Schools," was the following: "That the accustomary School Hours be duly Attended" (B. R., XIII, 53). After investigating "Complaints that were made against" Zachariah Hicks, the selectmen reported, June 12, 1758, "that the neglect of Duty complained of was not for want of Fidelity . . . but that it was occasion'd wholly by his Indisposition" (B. R., XVI, 14).

40 B. R., XII, 75.   41 B. R., XII, 108.

practice of Appointing a Committee for that Service." Instructions that they "Visit the Public Schools more frequently than has hitherto been Practic'd" suggest that the selectmen had been relying chiefly on the annual visitations.[42]

In spite of contemporary criticisms, it may be said that the public schools of colonial Boston were fairly well administered and supervised. An examination of the available records will convince one that the town was, at all times, attentive to their welfare.

[42] B. R., XIV, 233.

CHAPTER VIII
STUDIES

THE traditional program of the writing schools consisted of writing and arithmetic. Usually, these are the only subjects of instruction mentioned in the records. The ability to read was considered a prerequisite to entrance into the schools, at the age of seven. In reply to a "Complaint," John Proctor, master of the North Writing School, stated, at a meeting of the selectmen, April 15, 1741, "that he has refus'd none of the Inhabitants Children, but such as could not Read in the Psalter."[1] His practice, with reference to admittance, was not disapproved when it was reported at the next town meeting.[2] In some of the writing schools, however, the masters gave instruction in reading to those who needed it. At a visitation of June 26, 1738, the committee "inspected the Performances of the Scholars . . . both in Writing and Arithmetick, And heard the younger Scholars read."[3] On April 30, 1683, a committee "apoynted by the towne to consider of and provide one or more free schooles for teaching of children to write and cipher," voted that "Two schooles shall be pvided."[4] One school only was opened, November 1, 1684, at which the master was appointed to teach "Children . . . to read & write."[5] Ames Angier taught "Reading writing Scyphering," in 1722, at the South Writing School.[6]

In 1719, the selectmen voted "That the following directions be given to the Masters of the Free Writeing Schools within this Town vizt.

1. That morning and evening prayer be attended in the S^d Schools.

2. That a Portion of Gods Word be read by Some of ye Scholars morning and Evening by turns.

3. That the Schollars be Catechized every Saturday after the form of the Assemblyes Catechism.

4. That proper Seasons be Stated & Sett a part for the Encourageing of good Spelling.

5. That the accustomary School hours be duly Attended."[7]

---

[1] B. R., XV, 288. [2] B. R., XII, 279 (May 8, 1741). [3] B. R., XII, 213.

[4] B. R., VII, 161 (Apr. 30, 1683). On Dec. 18, 1682, the town instructed the selectmen to "consider of & pvide one or more Free Schooles for the teachinge of Children to write & cypher" (B. R., VII, 158).

[5] B. R., VII, 171 (Nov. 24, 1684).

[6] B. R., VIII, 164; XIII, 100 (July 11, 1722). See also B. R., XII, 108 (May 8, 1735): "Reading, Writing and Arithmetick."

[7] B. R., XIII, 53 (May 25, 1719).

Thirty years later, the town voted "that the Selectmen for the time be-ing, be and hereby they are desired to Recommend to the Masters of the Schools that they instruct their Scholars in Reading & Spelling and the Selectmen are desired to provide suitable Books for that Purpose at the Charge of the Town, to be given to such Poor Children as they may think proper."[8] So far as the records permit reconstruction, it may be said that, as early as 1719, the writing schools taught spelling, reading, writing, arithmetic, and the catechism.[9]

The town records contain but two references to the program of stud-ies at the Grammar School. Daniel Henchman was appointed "to as-sisst M[r] Woodmancy in the grammer Schoole & teach Childere to wright, the Year to begine the 1st of March 65–6."[10] Writing was taught at the school throughout the period during which it was the only public school in Boston.[11]

From the establishment of the first public school until the system was reorganized, in 1789, the entrance requirements at the grammar schools were the same as those at the writing schools. Boys were admitted at seven years of age, if they could read satisfactorily. Before 1684, some of the grammar school students who had not learned to write attended private schools, from eleven to twelve o'clock in the mornings, and from five to six in the afternoons, for instruction in that subject. The custom was continued, even after the public writing schools were opened.

The second reference to the grammar school program occurs in a "Memorial" which the selectmen "offered" to the town, March 13, 1710/11:

Whereas according to the information of Some of the Learned, who have made Observation of the easie & pleasant Rules and Methodes used in Some Schools in Europe, where Scollars p'haps within the Compass of one year, have attained to a Competent Proficiency So as to be able to read, and discourse in Lattin and of themselves capable to make Considerable Progress therein; And that according to the methodes used here Very many hundreds of boyes in this Town, who by their Parents were never designed for a more Liberal Education have Spent two, three, four years or more of their more Early dayes at the Lattin School, which hath proved of very Little, or no benefit as to their after Ac-complishm[t].

[8] B. R., XIV, 162 (May 9, 1749).

[9] Pupils of the time used a separate edition of the *Westminster Shorter Catechism*, as well as that which was appended to the *New England Primer*.

[10] B. R., VII, 30 (Mar. 26, 1666).

[11] From its establishment until Nov. 1, 1684, when instruction began at the writing school in Prison Lane (later Queen Street).

It is therefore proposed to the Town that they would Recom̄end it to those Gentle^m whom they shall chuse as Inspectors of the Schools, Together with ye ministers of the Town, To Consider whether in this Town (Where the Free School is maintained cheifly by a Town Rate on the Inhabitants) That Supposeing the former more Tedious and burthensome methode may be thought the best for such as are designed for Schollars (which is by Some questioned). Yet for the Sake & benefit of others who usually are the greater number by far in Such Schools, Whether it might not be adviseable that Some more easie and delightfull methodes be there attended and put in practice, And to Signifie to ye Town their thoughts therein, in order to the Encourageme^nt of the Same.[12]

The town records do not mention any subsequent action on these suggestions for reforming the instruction in Latin.

Cotton Mather, who was untiring in his "Concern" for the schools, must have known about the proposed reform. It may have been the inspiration for the following entry in his diary, March, 1710/11:

I am concerned for the Welfare of the great *Grammar School* of the Town. I would unite Counsils with a learned, pious, honourable Visitor of the School, to introduce divine good Intentions into it. This Among the rest; that *Castalio*, and *Posselius*, be brought into the School; and that the Lads for their Latin Exercises, turn into Latin such Things as may befriend the Interests of Christianity, in their Hearts and Lives;—particularly, the Quaestions and Answers, in our *Supplies from the Tower of David*.[13]

No doubt, Mather carried out his intention of recommending these works, but the town paid no attention to his suggestions. Castalio does appear among the texts used at a much later date, however.

The earliest known comprehensive "acct of the Methodes of Instruction" and the books used in the school, during the colonial period, appears in a letter of 1712, from Nathaniel Williams, the master, to Nehemiah Hobart:[14]

[12] B. R., VIII, 78. At this time, there were two public writing schools in Boston.

[13] *Coll. Mass. Hist. Soc.*, 7th Series, VII, 49.

Sébastien Châteillon, *Dialogorum sacrorum ad linguam et mores puerorum formandos libri iv*. Antwerp, 1552; Basel, 1557; London, 1565, 1573, 1580; Edin., 1698.

Johannes Posselius, *Syntaxis Graeca* . . . Wittenberg, 1561, 1568, 1586; Cambridge, 1640; *Apophthegmata Graecolatina* . . . *J. Posselii filii*, Frankfurt, 1616; and *Dialogues containing all the most usefull words of the Latine tongue* . . . London, 1623, are possibilities. The first two are recommended in Charles Hoole's *New discovery of the old art of teaching schoole*, London, 1660.

Cotton Mather, *The man of God furnished. The way of truth, laid out with a threefold catechism* . . . III. *Supplies from the tower of David* . . . Boston, 1708.

[14] The letter is reproduced in an excellent article on "The teaching of Latin and Greek at the Boston Latin School in 1712," by K. B. Murdock, in *Pubs. Colonial Soc. Mass.*, XXVII, 21–29.

The three first years are spent first in Learning by heart & then acc: to their capacities understanding the Accidence and Nomenclator, in construing & parsing acc: to the English rules of Syntax Sententiae Pueriles Cato & Corderius & Aesops Fables.[15]

The 4th year, or sooner if their capacities allow it, they are entred upon Erasmus to which they are allou'd no English, but are taught to translate it by the help of the Dictionary and Accidence, which English translatiō of theirs is written down fair by each of them, after the recital of the lesson, and then brought to the Master for his observation and correction both as to the Translatiō & orthography: This when corrected is carefully reserved till fryday, and then render'd into the Latin of the Author exactly instead of the old way of Repitition, and in the afternoon of that day it is (a part of it) varied for them as to mood tense number &c and given them to translate into Latin, still keeping to the words of the Author. an Example of which you have in the paper marked on the backside A. These continue to read Aesops Fables with y[e] English translation, the better to help them in the afores[d] translat[g]. They are also now initiated in the Latin grammar, and begin to give the latin rules in Propr: As in pres: & Syntax in their parsing; and at the latter end of the year enter upon Ovid de Tristibus (which is recited by heart on the usual time of fryday afternoon) & upon translating English into Latin, out of m[r] Garretson's Exercises.

The fifth year they are entred upon Tullies Epistles (Still continuing the use of Erasmus in the morning & Ovid de Trist: afternoon) the Elegancies of which are remarkd and improv'd in the afternoon of the day they learn it, by translating an English which contains the phrase somthing altered, and besides recited by heart on the repetition day. Ov: Metam: is learn'd by these at the latter end of the year, so also Prosodia Scanning & turning & making of verses, & 2 days in the week they continue to turn M[r] Gar: Engl: Ex: into Latin, w̄ the afternoons exerc: is ended, and turn a fable into verse a distich in a day.[16]

[15] Latin Accidences by John Stanbridge, John Brinsley, Charles Hoole, and Ezekiel Cheever were published before 1712. Very likely, Williams used *A short introduction to the Latin tongue, for the use of the lower forms in the Latin School. Being the Accidence abridged and compiled in that most easy and accurate method wherein the famous Mr. Ezekiel Cheever taught; and which he found the most advantageous by seventy years experience*, Boston, 1709.

Popular Nomenclators, at the time, were: *Nomenclatura brevis* . . . London, 1674, and *Nomenclatura brevis reserata* . . . London, 1676.

Cato's *Precepts*, and *Sententiae Pueriles, translated grammatically by John Brinsley*, London, 1622; *Catonis Disticha de Moribus* . . . *by J. Hoole*. Latin-English. London, 1659, 1670, 1704.

Many Latin and English editions of Corderius' *Colloquies* and Aesop's *Fables* had appeared before 1712.

[16] Erasmus' *Colloquia familiaria, de Copia Verborum,* and *Adagia* were all used, at this time, in grammar schools in England. The *Colloquia familiaria* appeared in an English translation by "H. M.," in London, 1671. A fly-leaf inscription, "Joseph Sewall Ejus Liber 1701," on a copy of the Amsterdam 1658 edition of the *Colloquia* suggests that Joseph Sewall used the book while under Cheever's tuition.

The sixth year they are entred upon Tullies Offices & Luc: Flor: for the forenoon, continuing the use of Ovid's Metam: in the afternoon, & at the end of the Year they read Virgil: The Elegancies of Tull: Off: are improved in the afternoon as is afores^d of Tull: Epist^1. & withal given the master in writing when the lesson is recited, & so are the phrases they can discover in Luc: Fl: All which that have been mett with in that week are comprehended in a Dialogue on Fryday forenoon, and after noon they turn a Fable into Lat: Verse. Every week these make a Latin Epistle, the last quarter of the Year, when also they begin to learn Greek, & Rhetorick.[17]

The seventh Year they read Tullie's Orations & Justin for the Latin & Greek Testam^t Isocrates Orat: Homer & Hesiod for the Greek in the forenoons & Virgil Horace Juvenal & Persius afternoons, as to their Exercises after the afternoon lessons are ended they translate Mundays & Tuesdays an Eng: Dialogue containing a Praxis upon the Phrases out of Godwin's Roman Antiquities. Wensdays they compose a Praxis on the Elegancies & Pithy sentences in their lesson in Horace in Lat: verse. On Repition days, bec: that work is easy, their time is improved in ye Forenoon in makeing Dialogues containing a Praxis upon a Particle out of Mr Walker, in the afternoon in Turning a Psalm or something Divine into Latin verse. Every fortnight they compose a theme, & now & then turn a Theme into a Declamation, the last quarter of the year.[18]

This program must have been approved by the town, and it may have

William Lily's *Propria quae maribus, Quae genus, As in praesenti, Syntaxis, Qui mihi construed* was often bound with his *Short Introduction of Grammar*, and *Brevissima institutio*, before 1712. John Clarke comments on this little text in his *Essay upon the Education of Youth in Grammar Schools* (London, 1720), 25–26.

J. Garretson, *English exercises for school-boys to translate into Latin, comprizing all the rules of grammar, and other necessary observations; ascending gradually from the meanest to higher capacities.* London, 1683, 1687, 1690, 1698.

Cicero's *Epistolae, de Officiis,* and *Orationes;* and Ovid's *de Tristibus* and *Metamorphoses* had also appeared in English translations before 1712.

[17] The *Epitome rerum romanorum,* by Lucius Annaeus Florus, had been translated into English by "E. M. B." (Oxford, 1636), and John Davies (London, 1667). A well-known Latin edition was the *Epitome in usum Delphinii.* London, 1692.

William Dugard, *Rhetorices elementa quaestionibus et responsionibus explicata . . .* 7th ed., London, 1673.

[18] Justin's *Historia* (an abridgment of Trogus Pompeius' history of the world from Ninus, founder of the Assyrian empire, to the reign of Augustus) and the *Satyrae* of Persius had also appeared in English translations.

Isocrates, *Orationes.* London, 1615, 1676.

Thomas Godwin, *Romanae historiae anthologiae. An English exposition of the Romane antiquities wherein many Romane and Englishe offices are parallelled and divers obscure phases explained.* Oxford, 1613, 1614, 1623, 1625, 1633; London, 1658, 1668, 1685, 1686, 1696.

William Walker, *Treatise on English particles, shewing much of the variety of their significations and uses in English: and how to render them into Latine according to the propriety and elegancy of that language. With a praxis on the same.* London, 1655, 1663, 1686.

been recommended, in the following year, for the North Grammar School.

In his eulogy of Ezekiel Cheever, Cotton Mather refers to the years when he was one of Cheever's pupils:

> A mighty Tribe of Well-instructed Youth
> Tell what they owe to him, and Tell with Truth,
> All the Eight parts of Speech he taught to them
> They now Employ to Trumpet his Esteem.
>
> .   .   .   .   .   .
>
> We Learnt Prosodia, but with that Design
> Our Masters Name should in our Verses shine.
> Our Weeping Ovid but instructed us
> To write upon his Death, De Tristibus.
> Tully we read, but still with this Intent,
> That in his praise we might be Eloquent.
> Our Stately Virgil made us but Contrive
> As our Anchises to keep him Alive.
>
> .   .   .   .   .   .
>
> And if we made a Theme, 'twas with Regret
> We might not on his Worth show all our Wit.
>
> .   .   .   .   .   .
>
> Grammar he taught, which 'twas his work to do;
> But he would Hagar have her place to know.
>
> .   .   .   .   .   .
>
> He taught us Lilly, and he Gospel taught;
> And us poor Children to our Saviour brought.
> Master of Sentences, he gave us more
> The [sic] we in our Sententiae had before.
> We Learn't Good Things in Tullies Offices;
> But we from him Learn't Better things than these.
> With Cato's he to us the Higher gave.
> Lessons of Jesus, that our Souls do save.
> We Constru'd Ovid's Metamorphosis,
> But on ourselves charg'd, not a Change to miss.[19]

All these are included in the account written in 1712 by Nathaniel Williams. Obviously, Mather had no intention of giving a complete list of his studies.

John Barnard, speaking of his early years (1690–91) at the school, says that Cheever "put our class upon turning Aesop's Fables into Latin

---

[19] Cotton Mather, *Corderius Americanus* . . . (Boston, 1708), 26–29. Mather probably attended the school from 1669 to 1674.

verse." He remarks, also, that he "was perfectly acquainted with pros-
ody."[20]

The "Books Benjamin Dolbeare Jun[r] learnt at m[r] John Lovell's
Latin School in Boston from 1752 to 1759" were the "Accidence ...
Corderius ... Aesop Fables ... Nomenclatur ... Clarkes Introduc-
tion ... Eutropius ... Dictionary ... Grammar ... Castalio ... Garret-
son's Exercises ... Tullies Epistles ... Ovids Metamorphoses ... Greek
Grammar ... Virgil ... Caesar Commentaries ... Greek Testament
... Latin Testament ... Terence ... Greek Lexicon ... Horace Delph
... Tullies Orations ... Kings Heathen Gods ... Gradus ad Parnas-
sum ... Homer."[21]

It is very likely that the course described by Nathaniel Williams was
followed until 1734, when he was succeeded by John Lovell. The
earlier program was then revised by Lovell, who preferred other authors
for the teaching of Latin and Greek, as Dolbeare's list indicates.[22]

A memorandum by Jonathan Homer, who attended the South
Grammar School from 1766 to 1773, contains the following account:

Entered Lovell's school at seven years ... We studied Latin from 8 o'clock
till 11, and from 1 till dark ... The course of study was, grammar; Esop, with
a translation; Clarke's Introduction to writing Latin; Eutropius, with a trans-

[20] John Barnard's autobiography, in *Coll. Mass. Hist. Soc.*, 3rd Series, V, 178–80.
Barnard was born Nov. 6, 1681. "In the spring of my eighth year I was sent to the
grammar-school ... after a few weeks, an odd accident drove me from the school ...
I spent a year and a half" at a private school, "and again I was sent to my aged
Mr. Cheever" (*ibid*, V, 178).

[21] A manuscript at the Mass. Hist. Soc. Another, with variant spelling, in the library
of the Public Latin School.

John Clarke, *An introduction to the making of Latin, comprising ... the substance of
Latin syntax* ... London, 1740. Many editions.

Flavius Eutropius' *Historia* had appeared in many Latin and English editions:
Historia, ab Anna Tanaq. Fabri filia ... in usum Delphini ... Oxford, 1696, 1703;
London, 1716; *Eutropii historiae romanae breviarium ... With an English translation
by J. C.* [John Clarke], London, 1722, 1728, 1744, 1750, 1759.

"Horace Delph" refers to the well-known Delphin editions such as the *Opera ...
cum interp. et notis P. Rodellii, ad usum Delphini* (London, 1690), or *Opera ... cum
notis L. Desprez in usum Delphini* (London, 1699, 1705, 1711, 1717).

William King, *An historical account of the heathen gods and heroes, necessary for the
understanding of the ancient poets* ... London, 1710, 1715, 1722, 1727.

*Gradus ad Parnassum sive novus synonymorum, epithetorum, phrasium poeticarum
ac versum thesaurus ... Opus emendatissimum* ... London, 1691, 1713, 1729, 1749.
Aler, P., *Gradus ad Parnassum* ... London, 1694.

[22] If Dolbeare's list is complete, Lovell omitted Cato, *Sententiae pueriles*, Ovid's *de
Tristibus*, Cicero's *de Officiis*, Lucius Florus, rhetoric, Justin, Isocrates, Hesiod, Juvenal, Persius, Walker, and Godwin. He added Eutropius, Castalio, Caesar's *Commentaries*, Terence, King's *Heathen Gods*, and the *Gradus ad Parnassum*.

lation; Corderius; Ovid's Metamorphoses; Virgil's Georgics; Aeneid; Caesar; Cicero. In the sixth year I began Greek, and for the first time attempted English composition, by translating Caesar's Commentaries. The master allowed us to read poetical translations, such as Trappe's and Dryden's Virgil. I was half way through Virgil when I began Greek with Ward's Greek Grammar.

After Cheever's Latin Accidence, we took Ward's Lily's Latin Grammar. After the Greek Grammar, we read the Greek Testament, and were allowed to use Beza's Latin translation. Then came Homer's Iliad, five or six books, using Clarke's translation with notes, and this was all my Greek education at School. Then we took Horace, and composed Latin verses, using the Gradus ad Parnassum.

I entered college at the age of fourteen years and three months, and was equal in Latin and Greek to the best in the senior class. Xenophon and Sallust were the only books used in college that I had not studied.[23]

The tale is continued by Harrison Gray Otis, who tells of the texts used during the years 1773–1775:

Gentlemen,—I send you as requested some reminiscences connected with the old Latin School in Boston. I was a pupil—first of Master Lovell, afterwards of Master Hunt. I perfectly remember the day I entered the School, July, 1773, being then seven years and nine months old. Immediately after the end of Commencement week, I repaired according to the rule prescribed for candidates for admission to the lowest form, to old master Lovell's house, situated in School Street, nearly opposite the site of the old School house. I was early on the ground, anticipated only by Mr. John Hubbard who lived near— it being understood that the boys were to take their places on the form in the same routine that they presented themselves at the house. The probationary exercise was reading a few verses in the Bible. Having passed muster in this, I was admitted as second boy in the lowest form.

I attended school from that time until April, 1775 (the day of the Lexington battle), being then on the second form. The school was divided into seven classes. A separate bench or form was allotted to each, besides a skipping form, appropriated for the few boys who were intended to be pushed forward a year

23 Fowle, W. B., "Schools of the olden time in Boston," in *The Common School Journal*, XII (Boston, 1850), 311–12. Fowle had Homer's copy of the manuscript catalogue of students (1734–1774), prepared by James Lovell, which is now in the library of the Public Latin School.

Joseph Trapp, *The Aeneis of Virgil, translated into English verse*. 2 vols. London, 1718–20; and later.

John Dryden, *The works of Virgil . . . Translated into English verse*. London, 1697; and later.

William Cambden, *Institutio Graece grammatices compendiaria . . .* Edited by John Ward. London, 1754; and later.

Théodore de Bèze, *Novum Testamentum . . .* Geneva, 1565; and later.

Samuel Clarke, *Homeri Ilias. Graece et Latine . . .* London, 1729; and later.

in advance. The books studied the first year were Cheever's Accidence, a small Nomenclature, and Corderius' Colloquies. The second year, Aesop's Fables, and towards the close of it, Eutropius and Ward's Lily's Grammar. The third year Eutropius and Grammar continued, and a book commenced called Clark's Introduction. In the fourth year, the fourth form, as well as the fifth form and sixth, being furnished with desks, commenced "making Latin," as the phrase was, and to the books used by the third form Caesar's Commentaries were added. After this were read in succession by the three upper classes, Tully's Orations, the first books of the Aeneid, and the highest classes dipped into Xenophon and Homer.

School opened at 7 in the summer and 8 in the winter, A.M., and at 1 P.M. throughout the year. It was ended at 11 A.M. and 5 P.M., at which hours the greater part went to the writing-school for an hour at a time—but a portion remained and took lessons in writing of "Master James," son of the Preceptor, and some young girls then came into the school.[24]

Together, the two lists for the period 1766–1775 agree substantially with Dolbeare's. Castalio, Garretson's *Exercises*, Terence, and King's *Heathen Gods* appear to have been discarded. The larger number of omissions in Otis's account may not be significant. Allowances should be made for recollections written in later life.[25] The fact that Jonathan Homer did not read Xenophon suggests that it was elective.

The "Books to be used in the respective Classes," according to a town committee vote of December 1, 1789, included all those listed by Dolbeare, with the exception of the Latin Testament and Terence, and the addition of the "Selectae e Veteri Testamento Historiae" and "Tullies Offices."[26] At this time, the Grammar School was "divided into four Classes."

The old seven-year program, begun at the age of seven, was very similar, and in no respect inferior, to the course offered at the best gram-

[24] Jenks, *op. cit.*, "Hist. Sketch," 35–36. The school year was twelve months, as at the writing schools.

William Lily, *A short introduction of grammar generally to be used . . .* 1st ed., London, 1574. Edited by J. Ward, London, 1732.

"Memoranda from an interleaved almanac for the year 1773, in the handwriting of J. Green," in Jenks, *op. cit.*, "Catalogue," 100, n. 1: "July 26th. I enter'd at Latin School and began ye accidence . . . Sept. 6. We began Nomenclator. 20th. Began in Corderius."

[25] Otis wrote the letter December 17, 1844, seventy-one years after he entered the school.

[26] *The System of Public Education Adopted by the Town of Boston*, 15th Octob. 1789 (Boston, 1789. Copy in H. C. L.), 3. The omission of a "Dictionary" and a "Greek Lexicon" (by Homer and Otis, and in the list of 1789) is not significant. Every pupil owned these books.

mar schools in England during the seventeenth and eighteenth centuries. It was designed to give the pupils a mastery of the Latin and Greek languages, and an acquaintance with some of the best authors in those tongues.

If Cotton Mather had had his way, the purposes of the writing and grammar schools would have been somewhat different. "Is there no Possibility for me to gett the Prosecutions and Operations of Piety into the Schools; that the Education there, may not only have Piety intermixed with it, but become the principall Intention of it? This would I make a Point of much Consideration, and be restless till I see a good Progress made in the Design."[27] As a matter of fact, the religious element played a relatively small part in the programs of instruction.

The purposes of the public schools of colonial Boston were adequately expressed in the report of a town committee, April 5, 1784: "they cannot on this Occasion, avoid expressing a Veneration for our Ancistors for their Wisdom, Piety and early Care in providing for the Instruction of Children, not only in Reading, Writing and Arithmetick which are Necessary to qualify them for common and ordinary Employments, but also in establishing Grammer Schools in which such of them as may be inclined may have the oppertunity of being initiated into a further Degree of Education, whereby they may be rendered more eminently useful to the Community as they successively enter upon the Stage of Life."[28]

---

[27] The Diary of Cotton Mather, entry of March, 1715/16, in *Coll. Mass. Hist. Soc.*, 7th Series, VIII, 341. See also *ibid*, 216, 226, 337, 345, 365, 451, 453.

[28] B. R., XXXI, 16. The grammar schools of Boston were not established or maintained as preparatory schools for Harvard College.

Appendices

APPENDIX A

SALARIES

MASTERS

	S.G.S.	N.G.S.	S.W.S.	N.W.S.	W.S.Q.St.
	Robert Woodmansey				
1650	£50				
	Ezekiel Cheever				
1671	£60				
					John Cole
1684					£30
1693	£60				
1697					£40
				Richard Henchman	
1701				£40	£40
1702				£40	£40
1703	£60				
	Nathaniel Williams				
1710	£100				
		John Barnard			
1713		£60			
					Jacob Sheafe
1714		£80		£60	£70
1715		£80		£60	£70
1716		£80			
1718	£150				£100
		Peleg Wiswall		Jeremiah Condy	
1719	£150	£100		£100	
			Ames Angier		
1720	£150		£100		
1723	£150				
1724		£130			
1726		£160			
			Peter Blin		
1727			£100		
1729		£200	£120		

	S.G.S.	N.G.S.	S.W.S.	N.W.S.		W.S.Q.St.
				John Proctor		
1731				£100		
1732				£160		
						Samuel Holyoke
1733				£190		£120
	John Lovell					
1734	£150					
1735				£240		£150
1736	£210					
1737		£280				
1738	£250			£280		£200
1741				£280		
			Zachariah Hicks			
1742	£300		£200			
			Abiah Holbrook	Zachariah Hicks		
1743	£350	£330	£200	£280		
1745			£300			
1746	£400					
1747			£380	£380		
1748	£600	£600	£600	£600		
1749	£600					
1750	£120	£120	£100	£100		£80
1751	£120	£120	£100	£100		£80
1752	£120	£120	£100	£100		£80
					Samuel Holbrook	
1753	£120	£120	£100	£100	£60	£80
					John Proctor, Jr.	
1754	£120	£120	£100	£100	£70	£80
1755	£120	£120	£100	£100	£80	£80
1756	£120	£120	£100	£100	£80	£80
1757	£120	£120	£100	£100	£80	£80
1758	£120	£80	£100	£100	£80	£80
1759	£120	£60	£100	£100	£80	£80
1760	£120	£60	£100	£100	£80	£80
				John Tileston		
1761	£120	£80	£100	£100	£80	£80
1762	£100	£80	£100	£100	£100	£80
1763	£120	£100	£100	£100	£100	£80
1764	£120	£100	£100	£100	£100	£80

	S.G.S.	N.G.S.	S.W.S.	N.W.S.	W.S.Q.St.	
1765	£120	£100	£100	£100	£100	£80
1766	£120	£100	£100	£100	£100	£80
		Samuel				
		Hunt				
1767	£120	£100	£100	£100	£100	£80
1768	£120	£100	£100	£100	£100	
			Samuel			
			Holbrook			
1769	£120	£100	£100	£100	£100	
1770	£120	£100	£100	£100	£100	
1771	£120	£120	£100	£100	£100	
1772	£120	£100	£100	£100	£100	
1773	£120	£120	£100	£100	£100	
					James	
					Carter	
1774	£120	£120	£100	£100	£100	

USHERS

	S.G.S.	N.G.S.	S.W.S.	N.W.S.	W.S.Q.St.
	Daniel				
	Henchman				
1666	£40				
	Ezekiel				
	Lewis				
1699	£40				
1701	£45				
1702	£45				
	Nathaniel				
	Williams				
1703	£80				
1704	£80				
1705	£80				
1706	£80				
	Ebenezer				
	Thayer				
1710	£40				
	Benjamin				
	Gibson				
1720	£50				
	Joseph				
	Green				
1722	£50				
				Zachariah	
				Hicks	
1733				£100	

	S.G.S.	N.G.S.	S.W.S.	N.W.S.	W.S.Q.St.
	Nathaniel Oliver				
1734	£80				
	Samuel Gibson				
1735	£100			£120	
1737	£125			£150	
		Jonathan Helyer			
1738		£90			
1741				£180	
			Abiah Holbrook		
1742			£180	£200	
				John Proctor, Jr.	
1743	£150			£120	
1745				£150	
1746	£200				
1748				£300	
	Robert T. Paine		Samuel Holbrook		
1750	£50		£50	£50	
	Nathaniel Gardner				
1751	£50		£50		
1752	£50		£50	£50	
1753	£50				
				John Tileston	
1754	£50			£34	
1755	£60				
1756	£60				
1757	£60			£50	
		Ephraim Langdon	John Vinal		
1758		£60	£50	£50	
1759	£60	£60	£50	£50	
	James Lovell				
1760	£60	£60	£50	£50	
1761	£60	£60	£50		
1762	£60	£60	£50		
1763	£60	£60	£50		
1764	£60	£60	£50		

	S.G.S.	N.G.S.	S.W.S.	N.W.S.	W.S.Q.St.
		Andrew Eliot			
1765	£60	£60			
		Josiah Langdon		James Carter	
1766	£60	£60		£50	
1767	£60			£50	
				William Dall	James Carter
1768	£60			£40	£50
1769	£60				£50
1770	£60				£50
1771	£60				£50
1772	£60				£50
1773	£60				£50
			Andrew Cunningham		Abiah Holbrook
1774	£60		£34		£50

The foregoing tables present the salaries which appear in the town records, exclusive of special or temporary allowances and grants made by the town. It will be noted that salary payments were made in old tenor during the years 1742–1749, a period of currency depreciation. The sources, listed under schools, are attached in chronological order to the names of the masters and ushers.

South Grammar School

John Woodbridge. B. R., II, 82 (Dec. 2, 1644): "Its ordered that the Constables shall pay unto Deacon Eliot for the use of m^r Woodbridge eight pounds due to him for keeping the Schoole the Last yeare." The constables were also collectors of taxes, rents, and fines. Obviously, £8 was not Woodbridge's total salary. Deacon Jacob Eliot was one of the selectmen.

Robert Woodmansey. B. R., II, 99 (Mar. 11, 1649/50).

Daniel Henchman. B. R., VII, 30 (Mar. 26, 1666).

Ezekiel Cheever. B. R., VII, 57 (Jan. 6, 1670/71), 215 (May 29, 1693); XI, 32 (Apr. 26, 1703).

Ezekiel Lewis. B. R., VII, 238 (Aug. 28, 1699); VIII, 7 (May 12, 1701); XI, 17 (Mar. 2, 1701/2), 27 (Aug. 31, 1702).

Nathaniel Williams. B. R., VIII, 29 (June 25, 1703); XI, 39 (July 11, 1704); VIII, 34 (Mar. 12, 1704/5), 37 (Mar. 11, 1705/6), 65 (Mar. 13, 1709/10), 133 (June 23, 1718), 139 (Apr. 29, 1719), 147 (Sept. 28, 1720), 170 (Mar. 11, 1722/23). I have included the temporary additions to Williams's salary, because they were continued from year to year, and were finally made permanent. See Samuel Sewall's letter to Increase Mather, Apr. 25, 1710, in *Coll. Mass. Hist. Soc.*, 6th Series, I, 391–93.

Ebenezer Thayer. B. R., VIII, 66 (Mar. 13, 1709/10).

Benjamin Gibson. B. R., VIII, 152–53 (Mar. 14, 1720/21).

Joseph Green. B. R., XIII, 100 (July 14, 1722).

Nathaniel Oliver. B. R., XIII, 248 (Jan. 9, 1733/34).

John Lovell. B. R., XII, 86 (May 21, 1734), 138 (Apr. 28, 1736), 189 (Mar. 14, 1737/38), 299 (May 11, 1742); XIV, 18 (May 4, 1743), 93 (May 14, 1746), 134 (Mar. 15, 1747/48), 177–78 (May 15, 1750), 199 (May 14, 1751), 212 (Mar. 10, 1751/52), 242 (May 28, 1753), 259 (May 15, 1754), 274 (May 16, 1755), 290 (May 11, 1756), 307 (May 10, 1757); XVI, 11 (May 16, 1758), 24 (May 15, 1759), 42 (May 16, 1760), 58 (May 12, 1761), 75 (May 11, 1762), 94 (May 10, 1763), 115 (May 15, 1764), 145 (May 14, 1765), 185 (May 26, 1766), 213 (May 8, 1767), 246 (May 4, 1768), 283 (May 5, 1769); XVIII, 23 (May 8, 1770), 57 (May 27, 1771), 81 (May 20, 1772), 139–40 (May 14, 1773), 180 (July 19, 1774). Shared £13/6/8 with James Lovell, May 8, 1767, for instructing North Grammar School pupils, "for about Six Weeks" after the resignation of Peleg Wiswall.

Samuel Gibson. B. R., XII, 101 (Mar. 11, 1734/35), 154 (Mar. 14, 1736/37); XIV, 18 (May 4, 1743), 86 (Mar. 11, 1745/46), 174 (Mar. 12, 1749/50): £100 old tenor "in full for past Services."

Robert Treat Paine. B. R., XIV, 178 (May 15, 1750).

Nathaniel Gardner. B. R., XIV, 199 (May 14, 1751), 213 (Mar. 10, 1751/52), 243 (May 28, 1753), 259 (May 15, 1754), 275 (May 16, 1755), 290–91 (May 11, 1756), 307 (May 10, 1757); XVI, 12 (May 16, 1758), 24 (May 15, 1759).

James Lovell. B. R., XVI, 43 (May 16, 1760), 59 (May 12, 1761), 75 (May 11, 1762), 94 (May 10, 1763), 116 (May 15, 1764), 126 (Aug. 16, 1764): voted £50 "as a Gratuity for his services," 146 (May 14, 1765): "Voted ... a further Sum of Forty Pounds ... as an encouragement," which was added every year until 1774. B. R., XIV, 185 (May 26, 1766), 213 (May 8, 1767), 247 (May 4, 1768), 283 (May 5, 1769); XVIII, 23 (May 8, 1770), 58 (May 27, 1771), 81 (May 20, 1772), 140 (May 14, 1773), 180 (July 19 1774). As indicated above, he shared £13/6/8 with John Lovell, May 8, 1767.

North Grammar School

Recompense Wadsworth. B. R., XI, 178 (Feb. 16, 1712/13); VIII, 93 (Mar. 9, 1712/13); XI, 181 (Mar. 30, 1713). Wadsworth's name does not appear in the table because he died within three months after his appointment. His salary would have been £60.

John Barnard. B.R., XI, 192 (Aug. 18, 1713); VIII, 101 (Mar. 16, 1713/14), 110 (Mar. 14, 1714/15), 119 (Mar. 12, 1715/16).

Peleg Wiswall. B. R., VIII, 136 (Mar. 10, 1718/19): "Voted. a grant of one hundred pounds for one year who Shall be Settled in and perform the Service of School master" at the North Grammar School. Wiswall was appointed, Apr. 29, 1719 (B. R., VIII, 139). B. R., VIII, 183 (Mar. 9, 1723/24), 196 (Mar. 15, 1725/26); XII, 7 (May 6, 1729), 167 (May 3, 1737); XIV, 8 (Mar. 16, 1742/43), 18 (Mar. 4, 1743), 134–35 (Mar. 15, 1747/48), 178 (May 15, 1750), 199 (May 15, 1751), 212 (Mar. 10, 1751/52), 242 (May 28, 1753), 259 (May 15, 1754), 274 (May 16, 1755), 290 (May 11, 1756), 307 (May 10, 1757); XVI, 11 (May 16, 1758), 24 (May 15, 1759), 42, 43 (May 13, 1760), 58 (May 12, 1761), 75 (May 11, 1762), 94 (May 10, 1763), 115 (May 15, 1764), 145 (May 14, 1765), 185 (May 26, 1766). On May 6, 1729, Wiswall was allowed £40 for an usher. He received grants of £100, Mar. 16, 1742/43; £200, Mar. 15, 1747/48; and £20, May 13, 1760.

Jonathan Helyer. B. R., XV, 133 (Sept. 7, 1738).

Samuel White. B. R., XV, 324 (Jan. 20, 1741/42): probable salary £90, which had been granted to his predecessor. B. R., XIV, 8 (Mar. 16, 1742/43): £40 old tenor "Added to his Salary."

Ephraim Langdon. B. R., XIX, 100 (Dec. 18, 1758); XVI, 25 (May 15, 1759), 43 (May 16, 1760), 59 (May 12, 1761), 75 (May 11, 1762), 94 (May 10, 1763), 116 (May 15, 1764), 146 (May 14, 1765).

Andrew Eliot, Jr. B. R., XX, 127 (Jan. 11, 1765).

Josiah Langdon. B. R., XVI, 185 (May 26, 1766).

Samuel Hunt. B. R., XVI, 213 (May 8, 1767), 246 (May 4, 1768), 282–83 (May 5, 1769); XVIII, 57 (May 27, 1771), 81 (May 20, 1772), 140 (May 14, 1773), 180 (July 19, 1774). Granted £30, Mar. 5, 1774, "to enable him to provide a House for himself the present Year" (B. R., XVIII, 159).

South Writing School

Ames Angier. B. R., VIII, 143 (Mar. 15, 1719/20). Very likely, his successor, Jacob Sheafe, received the same salary.

Peter Blin. B. R., VIII, 211 (May 8, 1727); XII, 4 (Mar. 10, 1728/29).

Samuel Allen. B. R., XII, 250 (Mar. 11, 1739/40): "Voted, That the Sum of Thirty Pounds p Annum, be ... Added to Mr. Samuel Allen's Salary." Total salary not indicated.

Zachariah Hicks. B. R., XII, 297 (May 11, 1742).

Abiah Holbrook. B. R., XIV, 18 (May 4, 1743), 65 (Mar. 25, 1745), 178 (May 15,

1750), 199 (May 14, 1751), 212 (Mar. 9, 1751/52), 243 (May 28, 1753), 259, 260 (May 15, 1754), 274 (May 16, 1755), 290 (May 11, 1756), 307 (May 10, 1757); XVI, 11–12 (May 16, 1758), 24 (May 15, 1759), 42 (May 16, 1760), 58–59 (May 12, 1761), 75 (May 11, 1762), 94 (May 10, 1763), 116 (May 15, 1764), 146 (May 14, 1765), 185, 186 (May 26, 1766), 213 (May 8, 1767), 246, 247 (May 4, 1768). Holbrook was granted £34 for an usher, May 15, 1754, and May 14, 1765; £40, May 26, 1766; £50, May 8, 1767, and May 4, 1768.

Samuel Holbrook. B. R., XIV, 179 (May 15, 1750), 199 (May 14, 1751), 213 (Mar. 9, 1751/52); XVI, 283 (May 5, 1769); XVIII, 23 (May 8, 1770), 57 (May 27, 1771), 81 (May 20, 1772), 140 (May 14, 1773), 180, 181 (July 19, 1774). He was allowed £34 for an usher, July 19, 1774.

John Vinal. B. R., XVI, 12 (May 16, 1758), 25 (May 15, 1759), 43 (May 16, 1760), 59 (May 12, 1761), 75 (May 11, 1762), 94 (May 10, 1763), 116 (May 15, 1764). Voted a grant of £30, May 11, 1762.

Andrew Cunningham. B. R., XXIII, 213 (Mar. 16, 1774).

North Writing School

Richard Henchman. B. R., XI, 4 (Apr. 28, 1701), 10 (Nov. 24, 1701), 17 (Mar. 6, 1701/2), 22 (May 25, 1702); VIII, 104 (May 14, 1714), 110 (Mar. 14, 1714/15).

Jeremiah Condy. B. R., VIII, 139 (Apr. 29, 1719).

John Proctor. B. R., XII, 27 (Mar. 13, 1731/32), 48 (May 28, 1733), 109 (May 7, 1735), 201 (May 17, 1738), 279 (May 8, 1741). Although his salary, on appointment, does not appear in the records, it is easily determined that he was granted £100 at that time. Additions of £60, £30, £50, and £40 make the salary £280, which is mentioned in the record of May 8, 1741.

Zachariah Hicks. B. R., XII, 40 (Mar. 13, 1732/33), 101 (Mar. 11, 1734/35), 170 (May 4, 1737), 279 (May 8, 1741); XIV, 4 (Mar. 15, 1742/43), 115–16 (May 12, 1747), 149–50 (May 10, 1748), 178 (May 15, 1750), 199 (May 14, 1751), 213 (Mar. 10, 1751/52), 243 (May 15, 1753), 259 (May 15, 1754), 274 (May 16, 1755), 290 (May 11, 1756), 307 (May 10, 1757); XVI, 12 (May 16, 1758), 24 (May 24, 1759), 42 (May 16, 1760).

Abiah Holbrook. B. R., XV, 351 (July 19, 1742).

John Proctor, Jr. B. R., XVII, 45 (Dec. 26, 1743); XIV, 65 (Mar. 25, 1745), 150 (May 10, 1748), 179 (May 15, 1750), 213 (Mar. 10, 1751/52), 259 (May 15, 1754).

John Tileston. B. R., XIV, 298 (Mar. 15, 1757); XVI, 12 (May 16, 1758), 25 (May 15, 1759), 43 (May 16, 1760), 59 (May 12, 1761), 75 (May 11,

1762), 94 (May 10, 1763), 116 (May 15, 1764), 146 (May 14, 1765), 185 (May 26, 1766), 213 (May 8, 1767), 247 (May 4, 1768), 283, 284 (May 5, 1769); XVIII, 23, 24 (May 8, 1770), 57, 58 (May 27, 1771), 81, 82 (May 20, 1772), 140 (May 14, 1773), 180 (July 19, 1774). Tileston was "Voted . . . the Sum of Thirty four Pounds . . . for providing an Assistant," 1761–65, 1769–73.

James Carter. B. R., XVI, 185 (May 26, 1766), 213 (May 8, 1767).

William Dall. B. R., XVIII, 181 (July 19, 1774).

The Writing School in Queen Street

John Cole. B. R., VII, 171 (Nov. 24, 1684), 227 (Mar. 22, 1696/97); XI, 3 (Apr. 28, 1701), 7 (July 28, 1701), 9 (Oct. 27, 1701), 15 (Jan. 26, 1701/2), 21 (Apr. 27, 1702), 25 (July 27, 1702).

Jacob Sheafe. B. R., VIII, 101 (Mar. 16, 1713/14), 110 (Mar. 14, 1714/15), 131 (Mar. 11, 1717/18).

Edward Mills. B. R., XII, 7 (May 6, 1729): "Voted . . . an Addition of Twenty Pounds." His salary was at least £100, the sum received by his predecessor in 1718.

Samuel Holyoke. B. R., XII, 41 (Mar. 12, 1732/33), 101 (Mar. 11, 1734/35), 202 (May 17, 1738); XIV, 178 (May 15, 1750), 199 (May 14, 1751), 212 (Mar. 10, 1751/52), 259 (May 15, 1754), 274 (May 16, 1755), 290 (May 11, 1756), 307 (May 10, 1757); XVI, 12 (May 16, 1758), 24 (May 15, 1759), 43 (May 16, 1760), 59 (May 12, 1761), 75 (May 11, 1762), 94 (May 10, 1763), 115 (May 15, 1764), 145 (May 14, 1765), 185 (May 26, 1766), 213 (May 8, 1767).

Samuel Holbrook. B. R., XVII, 299 (Aug. 1, 1753): "to be allowed Sixty Pounds p. annum, and also allowed to improve the School for his own advantage out of School hours, and to be entitled to the Perquisites of the School (the Fire money excepted)." The fire money belonged to Samuel Holyoke, the other master of the school. B. R., XIV, 259 (May 15, 1754): £70. Resigned before Aug. 9, 1754.

John Proctor, Jr. B. R., XIX, 12 (Aug. 9, 1754): "to be paid at the rate of Seventy Pounds lawful money p. annum, to be entitled to one half the Perquisites of the School (the Fire Money excepted) and also to have the improvement of the School out of School-hours." The fire money and the other half of the perquisites belonged to Samuel Holyoke. B. R., XIV, 275 (May 16, 1755), 291 (May 11, 1756), 307 (May 10, 1757); XVI, 12 (May 16, 1758), 24 (May 15, 1759), 43 (May 16, 1760), 59 (May 12, 1761), 75 (May 11, 1762), 94 (May 10, 1763), 115 (May 15, 1764), 145–46 (May 14, 1765), 185 (May 26, 1766), 213 (May 8, 1767), 246

(May 4, 1768), 283 (May 5, 1769); XVIII, 23 (May 8, 1770), 57 (May 27, 1771), 81 (May 20, 1772), 140 (May 14, 1773).

James Carter. B. R., XVI, 247 (May 4, 1768), 283 (May 5, 1769); XVIII, 24 (May 8, 1770), 58 (May 27, 1771), 82 (May 20, 1772), 140 (May 14, 1773), 180 (July 19, 1774). In every year from 1768 to 1773, he was "Voted . . . a further Sum of Twenty five Pounds . . . as an encouragement."

Abiah Holbrook. B. R., XVIII, 180 (July 19, 1774).

APPENDIX B

EZEKIEL CHEEVER'S DWELLING

*Agreement made between the Select men
and Capt. John Barnet vizt.*

That the Said Barnet Shall Erect a House on the Land where Mr Ezekiell Chever Lately dwelt of forty foot long, Twenty foot wide and Twenty foot Stud wth four foot rise in the Roof, to make a Cellar floor under one halfe of S^d house and to build a Kitchin of Sixteen foot in Length & twelve foot in bredth with a Chamber therein, and to Lay the floors flush through out the main house and to make three paire of Stayers in ye house & one paire in the Kitchin and to Inclose S^d house & to do and compleat all carpenters worke and to finde all timber boards, Clapboards, nayles, glass and Glaziers worke & Iron worke, and to make one Celler door and to finde one Lock for the Outer door of Said House, And also to make the Case^{mts} for S^d house, and perform S^d worke and to finish S^d building by the first day of August next.

In consideration whereof the Select men do agree that the S^d Capt Barnet Shall have the Old Timb^r, boards, Iron work & glass of the Old house now Standing on S^d Land and to pay unto him the Sum of One hundred and thirty pounds money that is to say forty pounds down in hand & the rest as the worke goes on.[1]

*Agreement made between the Select men
and M^r. John Goodwin vizt.*

That the Said John Goodwin agrees to do and perform the masons worke of the house now to be built on the Land where m^r. Ezekiell Chever Lately dwelt. S^d. house to be of the dementions agreed for wth Capt. John Barnerd. The S^d Goodwin to digg and Stone a Celler under the Largest end of S^d House, to under pin the whole house & Kitchen. S^d Cellar to be Six foot & four Inches deep under the Cell, the wall to be Laid with Lime and Sand Morter, to turn an Arch in S^d Celler and to build a good Stack of brick Chimneys, wth three Lower room Chimnyes two Chamber Chimneys and one garret Chimney, to fill Lath and plaster all the walls under the plate of Said house and Kitchen, to Ceile two floors through out the S^d House and plaster the Gable ends and under the Staires within Sight, and to plaster the Clossets and all the brickworke as high up as the Garret, to lay the Hearth of the Chimnyes with two rows of Tile in the Lower rooms and Chambers, and to plaster the Coveing, and to point the garret and Purge the Chimnyes with good Lime morter; and at the Said Goodwins Charge to finde all Stones, brick, Lime, Sand, Lath, Haire, nayles and other materialls for the Said worke, and to Compleat & finish the Same by the first day of August next.

In consideration whereof the Select men Shall pay unto the S^d John Good-

[1] B. R., XI, 11 (Nov. 24, 1701).

win the sum of Ninety pounds money, with the free Liberty of his useing all the Stones and Brick of the Old house now there Standing for his own use, and to have forthwith an order for Twenty pounds in part of paym[ts].[2]

Ordered that Cap[t]. John Barnerd do provide a Raysing Dinner for the Raysing the Schoolmasters House at the Charge of the Town not exceeding the Sum of Three pounds.[3]

Ordered that Cap[t]. John Barnerd have a noat for three pounds expended by him for a dinner at Raysing the Schoolmasters House.[4]

[2] B. R., XI, 11–12 (Nov. 24, 1701).
[3] B. R., XI, 23 (June 3, 1702).
[4] B. R., XI, 24 (June 29, 1702).

APPENDIX C

At a Meeting of the Selectmen, June 24^t. 1761.

Present

Thomas Cushing Esq.
Samuel Hewes Esq.
Benjamin Austin Esq.
M^r. Samuel Sewall
M^r. Ezekiel Lewis

Voted, that the Selectmen visit the Publick Schools in this Town, on Wednesday the first Day of July next, and that the following Gentlemen be desired to accompany them therein, Viz^t.

His Excellency the Governor
His Honor the Lieu^t. Governor
The Honble. John Osborne Esqr.
The Honble. Jacob Wendell Esqr.
The Honble. Samuel Wells Esqr.
The Honble. Andrew Oliver Esqr.
The Honble. John Erving Esqr.
The Honble. James Bowdoin Esqr.
The Honble. Thomas Hubbard Esqr.
The Honble. Thomas Hancock Esqr.
M^r. Speaker Otis
M^r. Treasurer Gray
M^r. Sheriff Greenleaf
The Gentlemen the Representatives
    of Boston
The Rev^d. Joseph Sewall D.D.
The Rev^d. Charles Chancey D.D.
The Rev^d. m^r. Pemberton
The Rev^d. Andrew Eliot
The Rev^d. Samuel Cooper
The Rev^d. Samuel Chickley
The Rev^d. Alexander Cummings
Richard Dana Esqr.
Thomas Barker Esqr. (Stranger)
John Ruddock Esqr.
Joshua Henshaw Esqr.
Joseph Jackson Esqr.
Ezek^l. Goldthwait Esq.
Andrew Oliver Esq.
Samuel Wentworth Esq.

Capt. William Taylor
Nathaniel Bethune Esq.
Joshua Winslow Esq.
Rev^d. m^r. Hooper
M^r. William Winter
D^r. Sprague
M^r. Oxenbridge Thacher
M^r. John Avery
M^r. John Box
M^r. James Perkins
M^r. Treasurer Jeffries
Belcher Noyes Esq.
Benjamin Pratt Esq.
Capt. Benjamin Hammatt
M^r. Alexander Hill
The Gentlemen Overseers of the Poor.

Ordered that M^r. Williston give seasonable notice to the several Gentlemen of this Appointment, and that they are desired to meet at the Town House at Nine Clock in the morning of said Day, and that he acquaint the several School masters therewith.

Voted, That there be a Dinner provided for the above Gentlemen on the Day for visiting the Schools.[1]

---

[1] B. R., XIX, 152–53. Seven selectmen, four representatives to the General Court, and twelve overseers of the poor were included among the sixty-six visitors.

APPENDIX D

SOURCES FOR ENROLLMENT STATISTICS

1738. B. R., XII, 213 (Mar. 19, 1738/39): visitation of June 26, 1738. B. R., XV, 133 (Sept. 5, 1738): Peleg Wiswall asks for an usher at the North Grammar School, because "the number of Scholars are lately increased." On May 6, 1729, Wiswall had been allowed £40 for an usher, because the school was "much Increased in the Number of Schollers" (B. R., XII, 7). See also B. R., XII, 193 (May 10, 1738).

1739. B. R., XII, 246 (Mar. 11, 1739/40): visitation of June 25, 1739.

1740. B. R., XII, 265 (Mar. 10, 1740/41); XV, 246 (June 25, 1740): visitation of June 23, 1740.

1741. B. R., XII, 292 (Mar. 9, 1741/42); XV, 299 (June 24, 1741): visitation of June 17, 1741. B. R., XII, 279 (May 8, 1741): "the North Writing School . . . consists of about Two Hundred and Eighty Scholars."

1742. B. R., XIV, 9–10 (Mar. 16, 1742/43); XV, 348–49 (June 24, 1742): visitation of June 23, 1742.

1743. B. R., XIV, 34 (Mar. 14, 1743/44): visitation of June 22, 1743. B. R., XVII, 19 (June 8, 1743): "Mr. Hicks informs that he has under his Instruction at the North Writing School One Hundred & Sixty Scholars." B. R., XVII, 22–23 (July 13, 1743): at the "South Writing School . . . One Hundred & Fifty Constant Scholars."

1744. B. R., XVII, 72–73 (June 25, 1744): visitation of June 22, 1744. B. R., XIV, 51 (May 9, 1744): the town voted to enlarge the South Writing School.

1745. B. R., XIV, 94 (May 14, 1746): visitation of June 25, 1745. B. R., XIV, 82 (Mar. 11, 1745/46): at the South Writing School, there were "220 Scholars which is near 50 more than were there last march meeting." B. R., XIV, 73 (May 3, 1745): "the Number of Scholars in the North Grammar School [is] so small . . . that there is no Occasion for an Usher."

1746. B. R., XIV, 119 (May 12, 1747): visitation of June 25, 1746. B. R., XVII, 139–40 (June 25, 1746): 550 for the North Writing School is a clerical error in the record.

1747. B. R., XIV, 149 (May 10, 1748); XVII, 165–66 (June 19, 1747): visitation of June 19, 1747.

1748. B. R., XIV, 162 (May 9, 1749); XVII, 197 (June 29, 1748): visitation of June 28, 1748.

1749. B. R., XIV, 177 (May 15, 1750): visitation of June 28, 1749. In the selectmen's minutes, it is June 23 (B. R., XVII, 223).

1750. B. R., XIV, 196 (May 14, 1751): visitation of June 22, 1750. B. R., XVII, 239 (Apr. 4, 1750): John Lovell asks for an usher, "as he now has a large number of Scholars to Educate." B. R., XIV, 179–80 (June 5, 1750): the Writing School in Queen Street to be enlarged, so that it "will then Accomodate One hundred and sixty or seventy Scholars, whereas it will now Accomodate but about Eighty or Ninety."

1751. B. R., XIV, 216 (May 12, 1752); XVII, 266 (June 19, 1751): visitation of June 19, 1751.

1753. B. R., XIV, 256 (May 15, 1754): visitation of June 29, 1753. B. R., XIV, 233 (Mar. 23, 1753): the South Writing School had "Two Hundred and Ninety Six Scholars." B. R., XXIX, 243: a "true List of Eighty-Six Scholars" at the Writing School in Queen Street, June 29, 1753.

No statistics for 1752 appear in the records. The visitation may have been omitted because of the "Small-Pox prevailing at this Time in the Town of Boston" (*Boston Weekly News-Letter*, June 18, 1752).

1754. B. R., XIV, 276 (May 26, 1755): visitation of July 5, 1754.

1755. B. R., XIV, 292 (May 11, 1756); XIX, 27 (June 30, 1755): visitation of June 27, 1755.

1756. B. R., XIV, 309 (May 10, 1757): visitation of June 25, 1756.

1757. B. R., XVI, 11 (May 16, 1758): visitation of June 24, 1757.

1758. B. R., XVI, 26 (May 15, 1759): visitation of June 28, 1758.

1759. B. R., XVI, 46 (May 13, 1760): visitation of July 4, 1759.

1761. B. R., XVI, 78 (May 11, 1762); XIX, 160 (Aug. 20, 1761): visitation of July 1, 1761. B. R., XIX, 147 (Apr. 29, 1761): John Tileston asks for an usher, at the North Writing School, because the "School is so numerous."

No statistics were reported for 1760. The visitation may have been omitted because of the smallpox epidemic at the time.

1762. B. R., XVI, 96 (May 10, 1763); XIX, 219 (Sept. 27, 1762): visitation of June 29, 1762. Supplementary statistics are recorded in the diary of John Tileston (*op. cit.*, 72): 1762, "May 7. 137 Boys at School at one Time in the Forenoon. May 10. 139 Boys present at one Time. May 17. 136 Boys present. May 18. 140 Boys present. May 19. 136 Boys present. June 14, 158 Boys present at once (afternoon). Aug. 23. 133 Boys present (exclusive of private scholars)" ... 1763, "May 11. 145 Boys (exclusive of P. School)." 1764, "Aug. 22. 147 Boys present, exclusive of private Scholars."

1763. B. R., XIV, 114 (May 15, 1764): visitation of June 29, 1763.

1764. B. R., XVI, 142 (May 14, 1765): visitation of "Tuesday the 10th. of June last," 1764. According to the selectmen's minutes, July 11, 1764, the visitation took place "on the Yesterday being the 10^t. of July"(B. R., XX, 84). The latter date is correct: in 1764, the tenth of June fell on Sunday.

1765. B. R., XVI, 181 (May 26, 1766): visitation of June 26, 1765. John Tileston notes in his diary, 1765, "June 2. The Select Men visited the Schools" (*op. cit.*, 72).

1766. B. R., XVI, 212 (May 8, 1767): visitation of June 25, 1766. See *Proc. Mass. Hist. Soc.*, XVII, 216–18: "List of the class which entered the South Latin School in 1766, and which closed its connection in 1773; in the order of entrance." Twenty-eight entered.

1767. B. R., XVI, 246 (May 4, 1768): visitation of July 1, 1767. The town clerk wrote "South Grammar School" for "South Writing School."

1768. B. R., XVI, 285 (May 5, 1769): visitation of July 6, 1768. The town clerk gave the "North Writing School in Queen Street 260 Scholars." The figure belongs to the North Writing School. B. R., XXIX, 318–19: a "Catalogue of Scholars at the South Writing School, the last Visitation Viz^t 1768" contains 200 names.

1769. B. R., XVIII, 25 (May 15, 1770): visitation of July 5, 1769.

1770. B. R., XVIII, 55 (May 7, 1771): visitation of July 4, 1770.

1771. B. R., XVIII, 79 (May 6, 1772): visitation of July 10, 1771.

1772. B. R., XVIII, 131 (May 5, 1773): visitation of July 1, 1772.

1773. B. R., XVIII, 168 (May 10, 1774): visitation of July 7, 1773. No statistics were reported for 1774 and 1775.

APPENDIX E

Addenda

TO PAGE 1, NOTE 3, AND PAGE 50, NOTE 45

The record of December 2, 1644 (p. 13, *supra*) suggests that Woodbridge became master of the school in 1643. Where he lived and kept school between 1643 and 1645 cannot be determined from the deeds or other records of the time.

On March 31, 1645, Thomas Scottow sold to the town "his Dwelling howse, and yard, and garden ... for the Towne use ... bounded with the Lands of Henry Messenger towards the North; with the Land of M^r. Richard Hutchinson towards the East [a large plot on the north corner of the present School and Washington Streets]: with the Common street [now School Street] toward the South: with the Burying place [now King's Chapel and burying ground] toward the west" (B. R., II, 83). The Scottow house, which stood near the present School Street entrance to City Hall Avenue (laid out 1839), was occupied by the schoolmaster, probably Woodbridge, as early as October 27, 1645. This is confirmed by the selectmen's minutes of that date: "It's Ordered that the Constables shall sett off six shillings of Henry Messenger's Rates, for mending the Schoole Master his part of the partition fence betweene their gardens" (B. R., II, 86). He may have kept school in his dwelling house.

Robert Woodmansey was living in this house on March 29, 1652, and teaching in a separate schoolhouse located about seventy feet to the west on the former Scottow land (p. 50, *supra*). The schoolhouse, erected by the town between March 31, 1645 and March 29, 1652, stood close to the present School Street facing the burying ground which occupied the north corner of the present School and Tremont Streets. The western end of the schoolhouse site is included in the rear (p. 3, *supra*) of the present King's Chapel (original building 1688, enlarged 1749).

Index of Names

INDEX OF NAMES

Addington, Isaac, 58

Allen, Bozoon, 6n

Allen, Jeremiah, 65

Allen, Samuel, 25, 85

Andros, Edmund, 6, 7, 8n, 44, 57n

Angier, Ames, 25, 64, 67, 79, 85

Armitage, Jonathan, 62

Austin, Benjamin, 91

Avery, John, 92

Ballard, Joseph, 61

Ballard, Robert, 41n

Balston, Martha Ballard, 41n

Barker, Thomas, 91

Barnard, John, 18, 19n, 31n, 52, 79, 85

Barnard, John (minister of Marblehead), 72

Barnard, Capt. John, 2, 3, 89, 90

Belcher, Jonathan, 60

Belknap, Joseph, 6n

Bellingham, Susanna, 12n

Bellingham, William, 12n

Bendall, Edward, 34

Bethune, Nathaniel, 92

Blin, Peter, 25, 65, 79, 85

Bowdoin, James, 91

Box, John, 92

Brattle, Thomas, 58, 59

Briggs, John, 29

Burroughs, John, 54n

Carter, James, 22, 24, 29n, 32n, 48, 49, 52, 83, 87, 88

Chauncy, Charles, 91

Checkley, Samuel, 91

Cheever, Ezekiel, 2, 7, 14, 15, 31, 41, 43, 44, 49, 51, 70n, 72, 74, 75, 79, 83, 89

Clark, John, 59

Clarke, Jonas, 62

Cole, John, 5, 7, 21, 51, 79, 87

Collson, David, 62

Condy, Jeremiah, 23, 65, 79, 86

Coney, John, 6n

Cooke, Elisha, 15, 58

Cooke, Richard, 43, 50

Cooper, Samuel, 91

Cotton, John, 36n

Cummings, Alexander, 91

Cunningham, Andrew, 27, 29n, 48n, 83, 86

Cushing, Thomas, 31, 91

Dall, William, 25, 83, 87

Dana, Richard, 91

Davenport, Addington, 15

Dolbeare, Benjamin, 73, 75

Dummer, Jeremiah, 2

Dunbar, Samuel, 16, 29n

Edwards, John, 65

Eliot, Andrew, 91

Eliot, Andrew, Jr., 20, 83, 85

Eliot, Jacob, 13, 83

Erving, John, 91

Fenno, John, 27

Fitch, Thomas, 59

Forsyth, Alexander, 62

Gardner, Nathaniel, 18, 82, 84

Gibson, Benjamin, 15, 43, 81, 84

Gibson, Samuel, 17, 82, 84

Goldthwait, Ezekiel, 91

Goodwin, John, 89

Gray, Harrison, 91

Green, Joseph, 16, 29n, 81, 84

Greenleaf, Stephen, 91

Gridley, Jeremiah, 16

Gunter, Thomas, 53n

Hammatt, Benjamin, 92

Hancock, Thomas, 91

Helyer, Jonathan, 19, 29n, 82, 85
Henchman, Daniel, 13, 31, 44, 49, 68, 81, 83
Henchman, Richard, 8, 23, 52, 79, 86
Henshaw, Joshua, 91
Hewes, Samuel, 91
Hicks, Zachariah, 23, 24, 26, 28, 30, 32n, 46, 47, 48, 52, 65, 80, 81, 85, 86, 93
Hill, Alexander, 92
Hobart, Nehemiah, 69
Holbrook, Abiah (the younger), 23, 29n, 83, 88
Holbrook, Abiah, Jr. (the elder), 22n, 23n, 24, 26, 27n, 32n, 47n, 48, 54, 56n, 80, 82, 85, 86
Holbrook, Elisha, 23n
Holbrook, Samuel, 22, 23, 26, 29n, 48n, 52, 53, 54, 80, 81, 82, 86, 87
Holyoke, Samuel, 22, 47, 52, 53, 80, 87
Homer, Jonathan, 73, 75
Hooper, William, 62, 92
Hubbard, John, 74
Hubbard, Thomas, 91
Hudson, Mary, 36
Hunt, Samuel, 11, 20, 28, 52, 81, 85
Hunt, William, 20n
Hutchinson, Edward, 8, 29, 31n
Hutchinson, Richard, 96
Hutchinson, Thomas, 8, 9, 29, 62
Hutchinson, Thomas, Jr., 62

Jackson, Joseph, 31n, 91
Jeffries, David, 46, 92
Jeffries, John, 62

Keayne, Robert, 36n

Lamb, Joshua, 37
Langdon, Ephraim, 19, 20, 29n, 49, 82, 85
Langdon, Josiah, 20, 83, 85
Langdon, Nathaniel, 20n

Legg, Samuel, 6n
Lewis, Ezekiel, 14, 44, 45n, 62, 83
Lewis, Ezekiel, Jr., 91
Love, Susanna, 8, 9n
Lovell, James, 18, 31n, 49, 82, 84
Lovell, John, 4n, 16, 17, 18n, 29n, 47, 51, 53, 61, 73, 74, 80, 84, 94
Lyman, Caleb, 62

Mather, Cotton, 7, 58, 62, 69, 72, 76
Mather, Increase, 6, 52, 58
Mather, Samuel, 8n
Maude, Daniel, 1n, 12, 31, 50n
Maude, Edward, 12n
Mears, John, 6n
Messenger, Henry, 96
Mills, Edward, 21, 51, 52, 87

Natstock, Joshua, 6, 7, 8
Noyes, Belcher, 92

Oliver, Andrew, 91
Oliver, James, 36
Oliver, John, 34
Oliver, Nathaniel, Jr., 17, 43, 82, 84
Osborne, John, 91
Otis, Harrison Gray, 4, 74, 75
Otis, James, 91

Paine, Moses, 35
Paine, Robert Treat, 17, 29n, 82, 84
Pemberton, Ebenezer, 91
Penn, James, 34
Perkins, James, 92
Pigeon, John, 3n
Pormort, Dorothy Dawson, 12n
Pormort, Philemon, 1, 12, 31, 33
Pormort, Thomas, 12n
Pratt, Benjamin, 92
Proctor, John, 22n, 23, 24, 28, 32n, 47, 53, 67, 80, 86
Proctor, John, Jr., 22, 24, 32n, 47, 48, 52, 53, 54n, 80, 82, 86, 87
Purkis, George, 6n

Robie, Thomas, 30
Ruck, John, 31n
Ruddock, John, 91

Savage, Habijah, 15
Scottow, Thomas, 96
Sewall, Joseph, 70n, 91
Sewall, Samuel, 2, 6, 15, 31n, 36n,
    37n, 38, 39, 41, 52, 58, 59
Sewall, Samuel, Jr., 91
Sheafe, Jacob, 21, 25, 41, 52, 79, 87
Sprague, John, 92
Stanley, Christopher, 36n
Stoddard, Anthony, 62
Sweet, Benjamin, 41

Taylor, William, 92
Thacher, Oxenbridge, 92
Thayer, Ebenezer, 15, 81, 84
Tileston, John, 8n, 22n, 24, 25, 28,
    29n, 30, 32, 48, 54, 80, 82, 86, 94,
    95
Tompson, Benjamin, 13, 49, 51
Townsend, Penn, 44, 65
Tyng, John, 3n

Vinal, John, 26, 28, 49, 54, 82, 86

Wadsworth, Joseph, 45n
Wadsworth, Recompense, 18, 29, 84
Ward, Joseph, 26
Wardwell, Frances, 61
Wells, Samuel, 91
Wendell, Jacob, 62, 91
Wentworth, Samuel, 91
Wheelwright, John, 12
White, Samuel, 19, 29n, 85
Wigglesworth, Edward, 15
Williams, Nathaniel, 2, 14, 15, 16, 17
    18n, 29n, 48n, 51, 53, 58, 69, 72,
    79, 81, 83
Williston, Ichabod, 61, 92
Wimburne, William, 34n
Winslow, Joshua, 92
Winter, William, 92
Winthrop, Adam, 59, 62
Winthrop, John, 33
Winthrop, Waite, 58
Wiswall, Ichabod, 30
Wiswall, Peleg, 19, 29n, 30, 32, 46n,
    47, 48, 50, 52, 61, 79, 85, 93
Woodbridge, John, 1n, 12, 31, 50,
    83, 96
Woodsmaney, Margaret, 51
Woodmansey, Robert, 1n, 13, 31,
    43, 50, 68, 79, 83, 96